DATE DUE

DEMCO, INC. 38-2931

THE
ABENAKI

THE
ABENAKI

Colin G. Calloway
University of Wyoming

Frank W. Porter III
General Editor

CHELSEA HOUSE PUBLISHERS
New York   Philadelphia

On the cover   Penobscot birch-bark plaque, about 11 inches high and 19 inches wide.

Chelsea House Publishers
Editor-in-Chief   Nancy Toff
Executive Editor   Remmel T. Nunn
Managing Editor   Karyn Gullen Brown
Copy Chief   Juliann Barbato
Picture Editor   Adrian Allen
Art Director   Maria Epes
Manufacturing Manager   Gerald Levine

Staff for **THE ABENAKI**
Senior Editor   Sam Tanenhaus
Assistant Editor   James M. Cornelius
Copy Editor   Terrance Dolan
Deputy Copy Chief   Ellen Scordato
Editorial Assistant   Clark Morgan
Assistant Art Director   Laurie Jewell
Layout   Victoria Tomaselli
Design Assistant   James Baker
Picture Researcher   Elie Porter
Production Coordinator   Joseph Romano

9 8

Library of Congress Cataloging in Publication Data

Calloway, Colin G. (Colin Gordon),
The Abenaki / by Colin G. Calloway.
   p.   cm.—(Indians of North America)
Bibliography: p.
Includes index.
ISBN 1-55546-687-7
   0-7910-0351-5 (pbk.)
1. Abenaki Indians. I. Title. II. Series: Indians of North
America (Chelsea House Publishers)
E99.A13C35   1989   88-25147
970.004'97—dc 19   ·   CIP

CONTENTS

INDIANS OF NORTH AMERICA

CHELSEA HOUSE PUBLISHERS

INDIANS OF NORTH AMERICA: CONFLICT AND SURVIVAL

Frank W. Porter III

The Indians survived our open intention of wiping them out, and since the tide turned they have even weathered our good intentions toward them, which can be much more deadly.

John Steinbeck
America and Americans

When Europeans first reached the North American continent, they found hundreds of tribes occupying a vast and rich country. The newcomers quickly recognized the wealth of natural resources. They were not, however, so quick or willing to recognize the spiritual, cultural, and intellectual riches of the people they called Indians.

The Indians of North America examines the problems that develop when people with different cultures come together. For American Indians, the consequences of their interaction with non-Indian people have been both productive and tragic. The Europeans believed they had "discovered" a "New World," but their religious bigotry, cultural bias, and materialistic world view kept them from appreciating and understanding the people who lived in it. All too often they attempted to change the way of life of the indigenous people. The Spanish conquistadores wanted the Indians as a source of labor. The Christian missionaries, many of whom were English, viewed them as potential converts. French traders and trappers used the Indians as a means to obtain pelts. As Francis Parkman, the 19th-century historian, stated, "Spanish civilization crushed the Indian; English civilization scorned and neglected him; French civilization embraced and cherished him."

Nearly 500 years later, many people think of American Indians as curious vestiges of a distant past, waging a futile war to survive in a Space Age society. Even today, our understanding of the history and culture of American Indians is too often derived from unsympathetic, culturally biased, and inaccurate reports. The American Indian, described and portrayed in thousands of movies, television programs, books, articles, and government studies, has either been raised to the status of the "noble savage" or disparaged as the "wild Indian" who resisted the westward expansion of the American frontier.

7

Where in this popular view are the real Indians, the human beings and communities whose ancestors can be traced back to ice-age hunters? Where are the creative and indomitable people whose sophisticated technologies used the natural resources to ensure their survival, whose military skill might even have prevented European settlement of North America if not for devastating epidemics and the disruption of the ecology? Where are the men and women who are today diligently struggling to assert their legal rights and express once again the value of their heritage?

The various Indian tribes of North America, like people everywhere, have a history that includes population expansion, adaptation to a range of regional environments, trade across wide networks, internal strife, and warfare. This was the reality. Europeans justified their conquests, however, by creating a mythical image of the New World and its native people. In this myth, the New World was a virgin land, waiting for the Europeans. The arrival of Christopher Columbus ended a timeless primitiveness for the original inhabitants.

Also part of this myth was the debate over the origins of the American Indians. Fantastic and diverse answers were proposed by the early explorers, missionaries, and settlers. Some thought that the Indians were descended from the Ten Lost Tribes of Israel, others that they were descended from inhabitants of the lost continent of Atlantis. One writer suggested that the Indians had reached North America in another Noah's ark.

A later myth, perpetrated by many historians, focused on the relentless persecution during the past five centuries until only a scattering of these "primitive" people remained to be herded onto reservations. This view fails to chronicle the overt and covert ways in which the Indians successfully coped with the intruders.

All of these myths presented one-sided interpretations that ignored the complexity of European and American events and policies. All left serious questions unanswered. What were the origins of the American Indians? Where did they come from? How and when did they get to the New World? What was their life—their culture—really like?

In the late 1800s, anthropologists and archaeologists in the Smithsonian Institution's newly created Bureau of American Ethnology in Washington, D. C., began to study scientifically the history and culture of the Indians of North America. They were motivated by an honest belief that the Indians were on the verge of extinction and that along with them would vanish their languages, religious beliefs, technology, myths, and legends. These men and women went out to visit, study, and record data from as many Indian communities as possible before this information was forever lost.

By this time there was a new myth in the national consciousness. American Indians existed as figures in the American past. They had performed a historical mission. They had challenged white settlers who trekked across the continent. Once conquered, however, they were supposed to accept graciously the way of life of their conquerors.

The reality again was different. American Indians resisted both actively and passively. They refused to lose their unique identity, to be assimilated into white society. Many whites viewed the Indians not only as members of a conquered nation but also as "inferior" and "unequal." The rights of the Indians could be expanded, contracted, or modified as the conquerors saw fit. In every generation, white society asked itself what to do with the American Indians. Their answers have resulted in the twists and turns of federal Indian policy.

There were two general approaches. One way was to raise the Indians to a "higher level" by "civilizing" them. Zealous missionaries considered it their Christian duty to elevate the Indian through conversion and scanty education. The other approach was to ignore the Indians until they disappeared under pressure from the ever-expanding white society. The myth of the "vanishing Indian" gave stronger support to the latter option, helping to justify the taking of the Indians' land.

Prior to the end of the 18th century, there was no national policy on Indians simply because the American nation had not yet come into existence. American Indians similarly did not possess a political or social unity with which to confront the various Europeans. They were not homogeneous. Rather, they were loosely formed bands and tribes, speaking nearly 300 languages and thousands of dialects. The collective identity felt by Indians today is a result of their common experiences of defeat and/or mistreatment at the hands of whites.

During the colonial period, the British crown did not have a coordinated policy toward the Indians of North America. Specific tribes (most notably the Iroquois and the Cherokee) became military and political pawns used by both the crown and the individual colonies. The success of the American Revolution brought no immediate change. When the United States acquired new territory from France and Mexico in the early 19th century, the federal government wanted to open this land to settlement by homesteaders. But the Indian tribes that lived on this land had signed treaties with European governments assuring their title to the land. Now the United States assumed legal responsibility for honoring these treaties.

At first, President Thomas Jefferson believed that the Louisiana Purchase contained sufficient land for both the Indians and the white population.

Within a generation, though, it became clear that the Indians would not be allowed to remain. In the 1830s the federal government began to coerce the eastern tribes to sign treaties agreeing to relinquish their ancestral land and move west of the Mississippi River. Whenever these negotiations failed, President Andrew Jackson used the military to remove the Indians. The southeastern tribes, promised food and transportation during their removal to the West, were instead forced to walk the "Trail of Tears." More than 4,000 men, women, and children died during this forced march. The "removal policy" was successful in opening the land to homesteaders, but it created enormous hardships for the Indians.

By 1871 most of the tribes in the United States had signed treaties ceding most or all of their ancestral land in exchange for reservations and welfare. The treaty terms were intended to bind both parties for all time. But in the General Allotment Act of 1887, the federal government changed its policy again. Now the goal was to make tribal members into individual landowners and farmers, encouraging their absorption into white society. This policy was advantageous to whites who were eager to acquire Indian land, but it proved disastrous for the Indians. One hundred thirty-eight million acres of reservation land were subdivided into tracts of 160, 80, or as little as 40 acres, and allotted to tribe members on an individual basis. Land owned in this way was said to have "trust status" and could not be sold. But the surplus land—all Indian land not allotted to individuals— was opened (for sale) to white settlers. Ultimately, more than 90 million acres of land were taken from the Indians by legal and illegal means.

The resulting loss of land was a catastrophe for the Indians. It was necessary to make it illegal for Indians to sell their land to non-Indians. The Indian Reorganization Act of 1934 officially ended the allotment period. Tribes that voted to accept the provisions of this act were reorganized, and an effort was made to purchase land within preexisting reservations to restore an adequate land base.

Ten years later, in 1944, federal Indian policy again shifted. Now the federal government wanted to get out of the "Indian business." In 1953 an act of Congress named specific tribes whose trust status was to be ended "at the earliest possible time." This new law enabled the United States to end unilaterally, whether the Indians wished it or not, the special status that protected the land in Indian tribal reservations. In the 1950s federal Indian policy was to transfer federal responsibility and jurisdiction to state governments, encourage the physical relocation of Indian peoples from reservations to urban areas, and hasten the termination, or extinction, of tribes.

Between 1954 and 1962 Congress passed specific laws authorizing the termination of more than 100 tribal groups. The stated purpose of the termination policy was to ensure the full and complete integration of Indians into American society. However, there is a less benign way to interpret this legislation. Even as termination was being discussed in Congress, 133 separate bills were introduced to permit the transfer of trust land ownership from Indians to non-Indians.

With the Johnson administration in the 1960s the federal government began to reject termination. In the 1970s yet another Indian policy emerged. Known as "self-determination," it favored keeping the protective role of the federal government while increasing tribal participation in, and control of, important areas of local government. In 1983 President Reagan, in a policy statement on Indian affairs, restated the unique "government to government" relationship of the United States with the Indians. However, federal programs since then have moved toward transferring Indian affairs to individual states, which have long desired to gain control of Indian land and resources.

As long as American Indians retain power, land, and resources that are coveted by the states and the federal government, there will continue to be a "clash of cultures," and the issues will be contested in the courts, Congress, the White House, and even in the international human rights community. To give all Americans a greater comprehension of the issues and conflicts involving American Indians today is a major goal of this series. These issues are not easily understood, nor can these conflicts be readily resolved. The study of North American Indian history and culture is a necessary and important step toward that comprehension. All Americans must learn the history of the relations between the Indians and the federal government, recognize the unique legal status of the Indians, and understand the heritage and cultures of the Indians of North America.

In this 17th-century engraving, New England Indians make maple syrup (foreground) and plant corn.

THE
PEOPLE
OF THE
DAWNLAND

Until recently, many Americans thought of Indians as war-bonneted horsemen galloping across a movie screen or as a forgotten people living quietly on western reservations. In the last few decades, however, these impressions have been revised. In 1969 Indian protesters made headlines when they occupied Alcatraz Island in San Francisco Bay. And in 1973 Sioux confronted federal marshals at Wounded Knee, South Dakota. But by and large, Native Americans seemed to belong to the past, especially in the eastern United States, where they were remembered only for their presence in the early days of the colonial era.

Then, on October 10, 1980, northeastern Indians came into the limelight when President Jimmy Carter signed into law the Maine Indian Claims Settlement Act. This law set aside $27 million in trust for 2 Indian peoples, the Penobscot and Passamaquoddy, and provided them with an additional $54.5 million to be used in buying back

300,000 acres of land in Maine. The total settlement—$81.5 million—was a compromise, for the Penobscot and Passamaquoddy had demanded the return of almost two-thirds of the land in the state. They argued that this land had been taken from them illegally.

The Maine Indian Claims Settlement Act was the biggest land settlement in the history of the U.S. government's dealings with Indian tribes. It was also an important milestone in federal Indian law. No less significantly, it occurred at a time when few Americans had ever heard of the Penobscot and Passamaquoddy or were aware that Indians still lived in Maine. Who were these Indians, and how had they managed to score such an important legal victory?

For at least 10,000 years and perhaps as many as 20,000 years before Europeans ventured to the New World, Indians occupied the northeastern parts of the present United States. One tribe living in northern New England at the

13

time of European contact was called the *Abenaki*. Their name—which means "people of the Dawnland" or simply "easterners"—refers to their nearness to the rising sun: Each new day the sun threw its first rays on the land of the Abenaki before continuing its journey west.

The inhabitants of this region called themselves *Wabanaki*, a more encompassing name that includes not only the eastern and western Abenaki but also the neighboring Passamaquoddy and Maliseet of eastern Maine and New Brunswick and the Micmac of Nova Scotia. Sometimes the various Wabanaki tribes joined together in a loose alliance known as a confederacy. Because the Passamaquoddy have often shared close connections and similar experiences with the Abenaki, they appear frequently in this story, especially in modern times.

The Abenaki were, and are, composed of two main branches. The larger branch, the eastern Abenaki, lived mainly in what is now Maine in distinct bands usually known by the names of the rivers they settled near. These groups included the Penobscot, Androscoggin, and Wawenock. In 1988, the most populous of these bands was the Penobscot, with about 2,000 members. (The neighboring Passamaquoddy, in eastern Maine, have about 2,500 members.)

Another branch of the Abenaki— the western bands—lived in New Hampshire and Vermont. These bands included several affiliated Indian groups. The Pennacook lived on the upper Merrimack River around present-day Concord, New Hampshire. The Winnipesaukee lived farther north, toward the White Mountains. The Pigwacket lived in the White Mountains, on the Saco River, near Fryeburg, Maine. The Sokoki and Cowasuck lived along the Connecticut River, and the Missisquoi and other bands were located on the shores of Lake Champlain, which straddles part of the New York–Vermont border and stretches into Canada. Today the combined population of the Vermont Abenaki is about 2,000. The Abenaki bands all spoke related dialects of a language known as Algonquian. They also shared many cultural similarities and historical experiences.

In the 17th and 18th centuries, as English colonists pushed onto their lands, many eastern and western Abenaki migrated north to Canada, settling in villages along the St. Lawrence River. One such community, located at Odanak (St. Francis) in Quebec, came to be known simply as the St. Francis Indians, even though their ancestors were native to Maine, New Hampshire, and Vermont; there is also a sizable community at Wôlinak (Becancour). The Quebec Abenaki today number about 1,000.

Other Abenaki remained in their ancient homelands despite great pressure to move, and today important Abenaki communities reside at Penobscot (Old

In Abenaki legend, Mount Katahdin, the highest point in what is now the state of Maine, was the roost of Pomola, a great birdlike creature who resented the arrival of mortals.

Town) in Maine and Missisquoi (Swanton) in Vermont.

Before Europeans arrived, the Abenaki homeland covered most of northern New England, from the Atlantic Coast in Maine to Lake Champlain in the west, where the lake waters formed a boundary between the lands of the Abenaki and those of the Iroquois tribes in New York State. From north to south, Abenaki hunting territories stretched from the St. Lawrence River to the Merrimack River and the northern border of Massachusetts.

This "Dawnland" is a region of mountain ranges divided by long rivers, a world of deep forests jeweled with sparkling lakes. In the east, the Atlantic Ocean breaks against the rock-strewn coast of Maine, and the Penobscot, Kennebec, and Merrimack rivers flow south to the sea. Streams flow west out of New Hampshire's White Mountains and east from the Green Mountains of Vermont to form the Connecticut River, which the Indians called *Kwini tekw*, "the long river." Impressive mountain peaks—Mansfield, Washington, Katahdin, and others—loom large against the horizon, and the Abenaki regarded some of them as sacred places where powerful spirits lived. To the west of the Green Mountains is Lake Champlain, more than 100 miles long. For the Abenaki it was a homeland, a border, and a place of spiritual significance—the Vermont Abenaki believed it was made by the mythical Odzihozo, "the Man Who Made Himself."

The lakes and waterways of northern New England provided numerous highways traveled by the Abenaki.

Some, paddling lightweight birchbark canoes, traveled long distances to trade, to negotiate with other peoples, to fight, or just to visit. Abenaki bands built villages on the banks of rivers, where there was plenty of fishing and fertile land for planting. Nearby, game-filled forests offered an ample supply of food for skilled Abenaki hunters.

Rich as this homeland was, its climate could be harsh. The Abenaki endured long, cold winters with frequent heavy snows and subzero temperatures. The harshness of winter, how-

The Abenaki, who often settled near rivers, built canoes of birchbark for travel, war parties, and fishing.

ever, gave way to beautiful seasons: Late spring and summer could be mild and pleasant, with clear air and cool breezes. And autumn was spectacular. The woods burst into a riot of colors, red and golden leaves blazing against the evergreen forest. Abenaki legend held that a star huntsman slew the celestial Great Bear and spilled his blood, which dyed the leaves in scarlet hues.

The Abenaki lived in small bands made up of linked families. Parents, grandparents, and children all traveled, settled, and hunted together. These family bands often congregated in larger villages to fish, plant the fields, hold ceremonies, or mobilize for war.

Like most Indians, the Abenaki referred to each band by the distinguishing features of the area it inhabited. For instance, some Penobscot lived at the "place where the river broadens out"; Cowass was the "place of the pines"; Missisquoi was "the place of the flint."

When the warm months came, the Abenaki spent much of their time gathering food. Because the climate curtailed the growing season, bands depended on hunting and fishing to provide the staples of their diet. A major spring event was the gathering of the Abenaki at the falls and rapids to fish for the smelt, salmon, shad, bass, and sturgeon that swam upriver to spawn. Fishing was so directly associated with spring that the Penobscot called April "spear-fish moon" or the "month of smelts." Spears were not their only tools. They also used nets and at night lit torches to attract their

The Abenaki fished from the shore with wooden spears. (Metal points, as shown here, were introduced by European traders.) In winter, this same tool could be used for ice fishing.

catch. A third method for catching fish was to construct weirs (fences or basketry enclosures) in the shallows. Abenaki built weirs at the outlet of Lake Winnipesaukee to catch mature shad making their way back to sea.

Fishing was not limited to the spring. During the summer, eastern Abenaki often went down to the sea to fish, harvest shellfish, and, sometimes,

This woodcut shows Indians cooking game on a grating that rests on four posts. What they did not eat right away they cured and stored for the winter.

hunt seals and other sea mammals. Inland Abenaki also went ice fishing in winter. They ate some of their catch right away; the rest was smoked and dried and eaten later in the year.

Late spring into early summer was also a time for clearing and planting the fields around the villages. May was "the planting moon." Abenaki in the valleys around Lake Champlain and the Connecticut River built their villages near fertile bottomlands, growing corn, beans, and squash, which they har-

vested in late summer and early fall. They also grew tobacco, an important plant in many Abenaki ceremonies. The Abenaki had no plows or iron and steel implements, but they made hoes and other tools from wood, bone, and stone. To supplement the bands' diet, women and children gathered berries and nuts. Acorns, beechnuts, walnuts, butternuts, chestnuts, cranberries, blackberries, blueberries, and raspberries provided a rich and varied addition. Nuts and dried berries were stored for winter along with corn, smoked fish, and dried meat. Abenaki women also drew sap from maple trees, collecting it in birchbark containers and boiling it.

Falling leaves and shorter days saw the bands disperse again. The men in each family hunted deer, moose, bear, beaver, and muskrat. The women cooked the animal meat and made clothing from the hides. The Abenaki also hunted waterfowl and the now-extinct passenger pigeon, which flew overhead in huge flocks on its southern migration. As winter approached, the Abenaki dug root cellars, which they lined with mats or birchbark and in which they stored corn and dried meat, sustenance for the lean months to come. Further nourishment came from the hunt. Men continued to stalk game during the winter months, wearing snowshoes made of wood and leather thongs that enabled them to chase down deer and moose whose hooves broke through the snow's crust.

The Abenaki killed only as much game as they needed—they never hunted for sport—and hunters revered the natural balance that existed between themselves and the animal world. They maintained this balance by regarding their prey with respect and by following rituals devised to avoid giving offense to an animal's spirit: A hunter who killed a deer or bear apologized to the animal's spirit, disposed of the bones properly, and did not waste any of the meat. In this way, the Abenaki believed, the species would

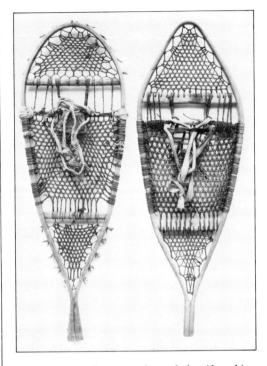

From leather thongs and wood the Abenaki fashioned snowshoes that enabled them to hunt moose, deer, and bear during the winter months.

survive and continue to provide good hunting.

The Abenaki considered themselves descended from animals and viewed their animal relations as "persons of other than human form." Family bands kept sacred totems or handmade emblems that showed their special relationship with a particular animal and its spirit. The people believed that members of the group inherited some of the characteristics of the animal of its totem. Bears, for example, were believed to be especially wise, and the Attean family, of the squirrel totem, were

This French document of the 18th century shows the animal totems used as signatures by several Abenaki and other tribes. Each family band had a sacred totem, or emblem, that symbolized the band's spiritual closeness with a specific creature.

thought to be bright, active people. In later years, Abenaki chiefs making treaties with colonists signed their agreement not by affixing their own names to the documents but by rendering an image of their family totem. Chief Orono, one of the most famous Penobscot chiefs of the 18th century, signed with the symbol of a beaver. Among the western Abenaki, a family emblem may

have indicated the importance of a particular animal to a hunting people rather than an association by descent.

Abenaki families lived in two different types of dwelling. The first type was the wigwam. It was conical in shape, made from hides or pieces of overlapping birchbark, and could be easily dismantled by a family on the move. The second type of dwelling, the longhouse, was larger, sturdier, and more permanent. The Abenaki built longhouses when they congregated in villages. Like the wigwam, the longhouse was built by Abenaki men, who erected a frame by cutting saplings, sticking them in the ground, bending the tops inward, and binding them to form a dome or an arch. Women then covered the frame with pieces of bark, sewing them together tightly enough that the covering formed a shelter from wind and rain. A French missionary who lived in an Abenaki longhouse in Maine in the 1600s described it as

> long and covered with the bark of trees of all kinds. The top is domed, with a hole over each fire to let out the smoke. The cabins are substantial and are made permanent and have six or eight fires according to the number of the family. There are some where thirty to sixty persons live.

Portable housing was essential to the Abenaki because the people moved regularly to make the best use of the many natural resources of their environment. The mobility of the Abenaki caused European colonists to call them "nomads." But the tribe was not simply itinerant. Groups moved with a purpose and obeyed a careful seasonal pattern. Moreover, the separate bands regularly returned to the longhouses of their central villages, and for several reasons—to strengthen their numbers during times of war, to hold social events, and to partake of a ceremonial midwinter feast. By thus alternating between movement and rest, the Abenaki avoided a problem that plagues more settled cultures: They did not exhaust the resources of a single region.

The Abenaki lived in a world fraught with peril, and they developed a rich mythology that tried to explain its dangerous forces. They believed, for instance, that when their fishermen drowned it was because they had been pulled under the water by monsters who inhabited the lakes and rivers. Hunters rarely ventured to the tops of the mountains for fear of offending the spirits who lived in those high regions,

A wigwam made of overlapping birchbark sheets attached to poles could be collapsed easily by a family or hunting party on the move.

and the Abenaki believed that Mount Katahdin, the highest mountain in Maine, was inhabited by a birdlike creature named Pomola, who resented mortals intruding from below.

The people did not merely submit to the forces ranged against them, however. For protection they turned to someone known as a shaman or *medeoulin*. The shaman—usually a man but sometimes a woman—possessed special powers and exerted great influence over the community. Shamans were believed to be closer to the spirit world than were ordinary men and women,

John Neptune, lieutenant governor of the Penobscot in the early 1800s, was a shaman as well as a tribal leader.

and they could enlist the aid of non-human helpers to provide spiritual guidance for the people. It was thought that shamans could predict and even control the weather and that they could cure the sick by their special knowledge of medicinal plants and herbs. They usually used their powers to achieve virtuous ends, but they might also use them for evil purposes. On such occasions they struck fear in the hearts of ordinary people.

Some shamans were also chiefs and thus attained tremendous prestige within the community. Passaconaway of the Pennacook, who wielded great influence in the Merrimack Valley in the early 17th century, was said to be a great magician. Another important 17th-century leader was Chief Madockawando, whose name in Penobscot meant "Wonder Worker." John Neptune, a Penobscot tribal lieutenant governor in the early 19th century, was also a shaman.

To European colonists, shamans were no better than "jugglers" or "medicine men"—sorcerers and conjurers. But, in fact, shamans performed a vital role in Abenaki culture, interpreting the spirit world just as European Christian priests interpreted the Bible and explained God to their congregations. And although Europeans dismissed Abenaki religion as "primitive superstition" or even denied that the people had any religion at all, in truth the Abenaki were deeply devout. Indeed, religion figured crucially in the daily life

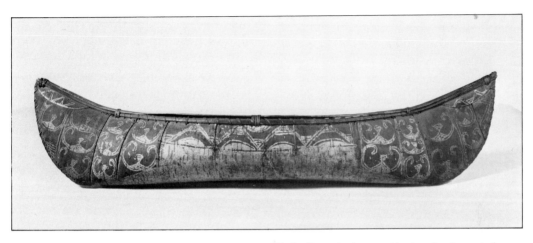

Birchbark canoes made by the Abenaki were sturdily built and often meticulously decorated with etchings.

of the Abenaki, who saw themselves as part of a pattern of existence that included the natural world.

The Abenaki celebrated their connection to the natural world in stories and legends handed down from generation to generation. These stories served three purposes: They entertained the people, especially on long winter nights; they preserved ancient memories; and, above all, they offered instruction. Like the legends of the ancient Greeks, or biblical stories, Abenaki lore helped teach people right from wrong and explained why the world worked as it did.

The Abenaki in Vermont believed that the world was created by Tabaldak, the Creator. But they also told the story of Odzihozo, "the Man Who Made Himself." Before he had legs, Odzihozo dragged himself around, gouging valleys in the land's surface and piling up

dirt with his hands to build mountains. Finally, he made Lake Champlain and, satisfied with his work, decided to stay there forever. Climbing on the rock in the middle of the lake, he transformed himself into a stone, and to this day he is said to inhabit Rock Dunder, just west of Burlington, Vermont. The Abenaki called it "the Guardian's Rock," and for generations they left offerings of tobacco there. They still consider it a sacred place.

Eastern and western Abenaki told similar tales of Gluskab, a mythical hero. He was said to have formed himself from the dust that Tabaldak brushed from his hands after he had finished making human beings. Tabaldak gave Gluskab the power to make the world a good place for the Abenaki to live. According to some accounts, however, he did not have free reign. He was opposed by his twin brother,

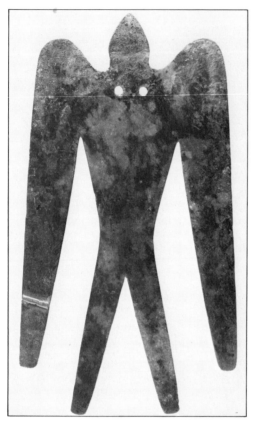

This copper ornament in the shape of a bird probably dates from the 17th century. It was found in an Indian grave in New Hampshire.

Malsumis, who went around doing evil until Gluskab killed him.

In one story, Gluskab is said to have learned that a hunter who killed or captured too many animals would destroy the balance of nature and cause his children to go hungry. To prevent this from happening, Gluskab visited Grandmother Woodchuck and asked her to pluck all the hair from her belly (which

explains, says the story, why woodchucks have no hair there). She then wove the hair into a magical bag. Gluskab took it from her and went into the forest, where he lured all the game animals—deer and caribou, moose, bears, raccoons, rabbits, and foxes—into the bag. Pleased with his achievement, he tossed the bag over his shoulder, went home, and displayed it proudly to Grandmother Woodchuck, saying they need never hunt again. But when she had looked in the bag, Grandmother Woodchuck scolded Gluskab. If he kept all the animals in a bag, she told him, they would die and the Abenaki would go hungry. Instead, the Abenaki should hunt the animals because it would help them keep strong. Gluskab saw his mistake and let the animals go free.

In another story—the tale of the Wind Eagle—Gluskab set out to capture the great bird that Tabaldak had placed on a mountain peak, where it generated strong winds by flapping its wings. Gluskab captured the eagle and bound its wings, and the winds ceased. Soon the air became so hot and heavy that Gluskab could not breathe. He restored the eagle to its lofty perch and loosened its wings so that it could make enough wind to cool the people and the animals.

Yet another story tells how Gluskab saved the plants and animals that were dying of thirst because all the earth's water was held in the belly of a huge froglike creature. Gluskab slew the monster and released the water, which formed streams and rivers. In their relief, many animals leaped into the water and turned into fish and water creatures. Still other tales related how Gluskab brought the people tobacco and canoes.

The deeds of Gluskab and other stories about the world's creation served to affirm the harmonious relationship between the Abenaki and their universe. But this harmony was disrupted when Europeans arrived in North America. Some Abenaki believed Gluskab was enraged by the treachery of these newcomers, who evidently had not learned the lessons he taught. Towns and farms ate into the forests; mills and highways polluted the air and streams. The balance between humanity and nature that the Abenaki had maintained for so long was destroyed. Gluskab departed in anger. Thereafter the Abenaki were unprotected, and the way was opened for the suffering and hardship of the years to come. ▲

This close-up shows an old woman weaving a basket. Enormous care still goes into such craftwork.

SOCIETY, ART,
AND
CULTURE

What was life like for the people of the Dawnland? What could young Abenaki expect from life as they came of age? What, in turn, was expected of them as they took their place as young men and women in Abenaki society?

The seasonal cycle of hunting, fishing, planting, harvesting, and gathering occupied much of the Abenakis' time and energies, but they also developed a culture rich in family relations, social activities, song, and ceremony. Growing up in this world shaped the character of young Abenaki and prepared them for the roles they would perform as adults.

Immediately after birth, Abenaki babies were bound to a cradleboard that the mother carried on her back. When she performed chores, the mother either hung the cradleboard from a branch or placed her child in a small hammock, padded with moss, to keep it out of harm's way.

The newborn baby entered a world in which family relationships mattered a great deal. The ties between members of the family were close, and family unity was vital. Abenaki children grew up surrounded by parents, grandparents, aunts and uncles, sisters and brothers, and cousins. Family members shared food, possessions, good times, and hardship. Cousins were close and addressed each other as brother or sister. Aunts and uncles played a large role in raising Abenaki children. Custom called for them to adopt orphaned nieces and nephews or to share the task of raising them with the children's grandparents. Children repaid the debt by caring for their elders when they reached old age.

Abenaki society attached great importance to sharing, generosity, and hospitality. These virtues could mean the difference between eating and going hungry. In good times and bad, the family band ate communal meals, and no one went hungry while his neighbors feasted. The young Abenaki growing up in this society were taught that concern for others should always be shown and that a selfish person was

A Penobscot mother places her baby in a hammock, 1911. Hammocks kept infants safely off the ground while their mother worked.

of no use to the community. Hunters won as much admiration for their generosity as for their skill with the bow and arrow.

Abenaki children treated their elders with great respect, and the elders showed kindness to children. Adults preferred teaching to punishment. The young learned from their parents, aunts and uncles, and other elders. And they drank in the wisdom of the tales they heard around winter hearth fires.

Young Abenaki learned that their culture frowned upon outbursts of an-

ger and loud behavior and that it treasured restraint and self-control. Quiet, polite, and considerate behavior helped maintain harmonious relations in a society that valued cooperation and mutual concern. Abenaki who fought and argued brought shame on themselves, and children who threw fits of temper earned only the disapproval of their family.

When Europeans first met the Abenaki, they expected to find Indian societies governed like European countries—by kings and queens. Sometimes they called Indian chiefs "kings"; more often they said the Indians had no real form of government. In fact, the elected chiefs, or sagamores, of the Abenaki generally held their position for life, but they had only limited authority and could be deposed if they behaved badly or if the band suffered misfortune under their leadership. Nor did Abenaki chiefs always wield great influence. Some did, but for the most part the Abenaki were governed by custom and by the force of public opinion rather than by strong leaders. The sagamore's influence stemmed from his skill as a hunter, his bravery as a warrior, his power as an orator, and his reputation for honesty, generosity, and wisdom. One of the chief's most important tasks was settling differences between band members. He did this not through force but through negotiation.

Various Abenaki groups often formed alliances, but they recognized no single, supreme chief. Indeed, civil or peace chiefs had separate functions and powers from war captains. These men, too, were raised up to their position by the consensus of the tribe.

Under normal circumstances, the ties between families, not written laws or the command of its leaders, held Abenaki society together. When a major decision had to be made, all the band's members—men, women, even children—had the chance to speak in council, and the advice of old people was treated with particular respect. Afterward, the group arrived at a general agreement.

Abenaki children played with dolls made from corn husks and corn silk, as well as a variety of other toys and games.

Despite the rigors of Abenaki society, there was plenty of opportunity for fun and relaxation. The people often sang and told stories as they went about their daily chores; riddles and word games were also popular. The routine of snaring and preparing food was lightened by lively ceremonies and feasts.

The Abenaki also enjoyed sports. One sport, lacrosse, was played on a long field. Players raced up and down it, wielding sticks with small baskets attached for throwing and catching a hard ball and hurling it into a net. Lacrosse

THE ORIGIN OF CORN

A long time ago, when Indians were first made, there lived one alone, far, far from any others. He knew not of fire, and subsisted on roots, bark, and nuts. This Indian became very lonesome for company. He grew tired of digging roots, lost his appetite, and for several days lay dreaming in the sunshine; when he awoke he saw something standing near, at which, at first, he was very much frightened. But when it spoke, his heart was glad, for it was a beautiful woman with long *light* hair, very unlike any Indian. He asked her to come to him, but she would not, and if he tried to approach her she seemed to go farther away; he sang to her of his loneliness and besought her not to leave him; at last she told him, if he would do just as she would say, he would always have her with him. He promised that he would.

She led him to where there was some very dry grass, told him to get two very dry sticks, rub them together quickly, holding them in the grass. Soon a spark flew out; the grass caught it, and quick as an arrow the ground was burned over. Then she said, "When the sun sets, take me by the hair and drag me over the burned ground." He did not like to do this, but she told him that wherever he dragged her something like grass would spring up, and he would see her hair coming from between the leaves; then the seeds would be ready for his use. He did as she said, and to this day, when they see silk (hair) on the cornstalk, the Indians know she has not forgotten them.

(From *Tales of the North American Indians*. Selected and edited by Stith Thompson. Cambridge, MA: Harvard University Press, 1929.)

remains popular—among Indians and whites alike—in many parts of North America. In Abenaki culture, it was mainly played by adult men. Children had their own activities, including play with corn-husk dolls, dice, and the game of pin and bundles. The object of this game was to toss a bundle of moose hair and cedar twigs into the air and catch it on a stick. Another popular pas-time involved a smooth rod—called a *snowsnake*—made of a carved piece of hardwood such as hickory, with a rounded head slightly turned up at one end. Players sent the snake skidding along a cleared strip of smooth, packed snow. The winner was the player who slid his snake the farthest.

Abenaki society was divided along gender lines. Men and women had different duties and responsibilities. The men carried out strenuous and dangerous tasks of hunting and warfare, as well as cutting down trees, erecting the frames of longhouses, and building canoes. Women's tasks kept them closer to home, tending the crops in the fields near the village, cooking, making birch baskets and bowls, tanning hides, and sewing and decorating clothing. Because of the seriousness and difficulty of these tasks, the children's education had to begin early, to prepare boys and girls for the life they would lead as an adult.

At a very early age, boys and girls studied the skills required of them by the tribe. Boys began to practice with the bow and arrow almost as soon as they could walk; an adept 10- or 12-year-old could kill a bird with his arrow. Boys accompanied their father and uncles on hunting and fishing trips and learned how to use the bow and spear, how to imitate birdcalls and animal sounds, how to disguise and conceal themselves from the prey, and how to wait patiently until the right moment came. Here again, self-control was vital. Running, swimming, and wrestling also helped develop a youth's muscles and agility. The fleetest young Abenaki were trained to run a deer or moose to ground after a chase that often covered several miles.

A young man also undertook a vision quest, in the hope of acquiring a guardian spirit who would help and protect him through life. The first step

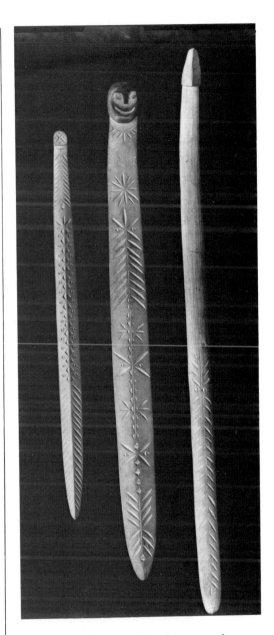

In snowsnakes, *an Abenaki game, players compete by skidding a piece of carved wood as far as possible atop smooth snow. These three snakes were made by Penobscot.*

Boys accompanied their fathers on hunting expeditions as soon as they could shoot a bow and arrow. Tadpole-shaped snowshoes gave the hunter more agility than did the larger, rounder models.

was for the boy to fast and thereby purify himself. He then went off alone to a remote place, where he waited for a guardian helper to appear in a vision or dream, perhaps in the form of an eagle, a bear, or a turtle. The youth then could feel confident in the knowledge that his guardian spirit would aid him with its special powers. By the time he was 14 or 15 years old, a young Abenaki was ready to take his place in society as a hunter, warrior, provider, and protector. If he was successful and earned the admiration and respect of his people,

he might someday reach the exalted status of chief.

Girls, meanwhile, accompanied the women in their tasks. Many of these activities were communal, such as gathering maple syrup, planting the fields, taking in the harvest, and weaving baskets. Women and girls made clay pottery and birchbark and wooden containers, and they also prepared the family's meals. They cooked by placing vessels directly over a fire or by dropping heated stones into the water in which the food was cooking.

Women and girls made most of the clothing for the band. Using wooden, bone, or stone scrapers, awls, and needles, girls learned to tan hides and make clothes. They learned to decorate garments with dyes or with embroidery and other quill work. People dressed lightly during the warm summer months, but with the coming of winter the Abenaki donned furs, hides, and leggings to keep them warm. In the 1720s, Father Sebastian Rasles, a Jesuit missionary from France, described in his journal the winter attire of the Abenaki:

The clothing of the men consists of a loose coat of skin, or a piece of red or blue cloth. That of the women is a covering which extends from the neck to the middle of the leg, and which they adjust very delicately. They put on the head another covering which descends as far as the feet, and serves them as a cloak. Their leggings reach from the knee only to the ankle. Socks made of elk-skin, and lined inside with hair or with wool, take the place of shoes. This foot-gear is absolutely necessary for the purpose of adjusting their snowshoes, by means of which they walk easily on the snow.

The "socks" Father Rasles mentions were in fact moccasins, usually made of three pieces of skin: one for the sole and sides, one for the top and tongue, and one piece that wrapped around the ankle. Men and women wore shirts, and their coats were sometimes beautifully embroidered and decorated. Like the women, Abenaki men also sometimes wore conical caps, especially when they were hunting, for tradition's sake. Women's jewelry included strings of shells or beads tied in their hair, which they wore long and either wrapped in a headband, tied in braids, or coiled on top of their head.

By today's standards, the life of Abenaki women seems hard, but it was probably no more taxing than the lives of most women of their time. Abenaki women had their share of leisure and relaxation, which included the chatting and singing they enjoyed while doing

This knife has a nine-inch sheath made from moose hide and a handle made of bone.

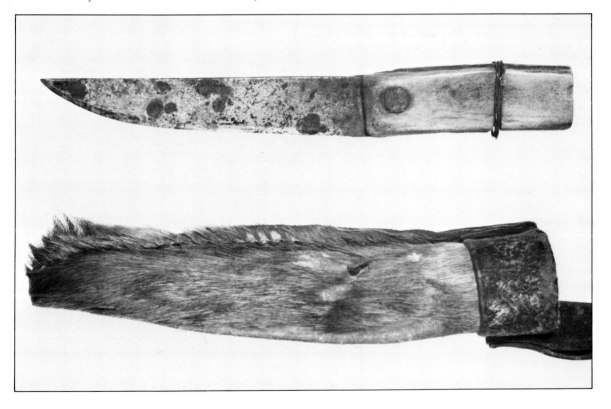

the communal tasks. All in all, they were treated with respect; as in many Indian societies, the Abenaki used *mother* and *grandmother* as terms of honor.

A crucial time in the life of an Abenaki girl was the onset of menstruation. It signaled the arrival of womanhood. Like many Indian peoples, the Abenaki viewed this development as a special occasion. Menstruating women were given a special wigwam, separate from the band. They could not cook for their men or come into contact with them during this period for fear they might contaminate and weaken the men.

Once a girl reached physical maturity, she was ready for marriage. In Abenaki society, marriage created ties between families and strengthened the bonds that held mobile bands together. Restrictions governed one's choice of a spouse. Close cousins were not permitted to marry, and a young man had to demonstrate his proficiency as a provider. Today, the Penobscot recall that in the old days, a young man who sought a girl's hand in marriage needed

In the 17th century, a Pennacook Indian decorated this leather pouch with shells and porcupine quills.

only to toss a chip of wood in her direction as a sign of his intentions. If the girl picked up the piece of wood, it meant she had accepted his proposal. In more recent times, a young man usually asked an uncle or an elder to act as a go-between whose task was to take a gift to the girl's family. If the family accepted the gift, they accepted the proposal of marriage. Sometimes, however, negotiations between families could be prolonged. The wedding ceremony itself was accompanied by a feast and dance, and the couple agreed to "live together always."

After the marriage, the new son-in-law normally took up residence with his wife's family, although a western Abenaki bride sometimes moved in with her husband's family. The new couple joined the family band and in time produced a family of their own. They were now adults and thus expected to care for their aging parents as well as for their own children. They also helped raise and educate the other children in the band, especially their nieces and nephews.

As the couple aged, they in turn were cared for by younger members of the family band. Life expectancy probably was about 40 years—a short span by modern standards but typical of most societies before the 19th century. In fact, there is evidence that the Abenaki diet was better than that of most non-Indians of the time. Some Abenaki lived to 80 or 90 years of age.

When death came, relatives clothed the deceased in his or her finest garments and wrapped the body in a roll made of birchbark. The relatives buried the body along with personal possessions that the departed person had especially valued. In wintertime, when the ground was frozen, corpses were placed on a scaffold until the spring thaw. The burial ceremony included a funeral song chanted by the band. Then came a period of mourning. The widow mourned for a year, wearing a hood as a sign of grief; a widower painted his face black. In their bereavement, widows and widowers turned to members of the family band for comfort.

Just as ceremonies helped ease the pain of death, so art added luster to life. Even after whites had forever damaged Abenaki society, Abenaki artists continued to produce works of great beauty that reflected the richness of their cultural heritage and the survival of traditional beliefs and meanings. Non-Indians often distinguish "traditional" Indian art from the more recent art that shows the influence of contact with Europeans. But the distinction is not so clear. Indian art and culture has always undergone change, as artisans responded to new influences, employed new techniques, and incorporated new designs. For instance, after European traders came to the Dawnland in the 17th century, the Abenaki began to use metal knives, cloth (instead of skins), and decorative glass beads (instead of shells or porcupine quills). These new objects—no less than the old—helped the Abenaki add beauty and definition to their life.

These birch boxes held castor, *the oily, foul-smelling beaver scent used by hunters to attract animals. The containers had to be perfectly fitted and sealed.*

In addition to making decorative items, the Abenaki fashioned tools, vessels, and other implements. Their favorite medium was the bark that grew on the white birch trees that filled the forests of northern New England. Birchbark can be separated into thin sheets so flexible, waterproof, and durable that the Abenaki continued to use the bark long after metal utensils became available from traders. Bark could be shaped into baskets, cups and bowls, boxes, kettles, cooking utensils, cradles, canoes, wigwams, mats, and a host of other items.

Not only were these objects useful; they also attained the beauty of finished works of art. Abenaki craft workers scraped away the surface of the birchbark and exposed the inner bark, which was another shade. The contrast inspired artisans to etch delicate patterns on birchbark boxes, cradles, and canoes. Sometimes they scratched a light pattern on a dark background, known as "negative etching," or a dark pattern on a light background, known as "positive etching." When the Abenaki got metal tools from European traders, they etched more intricate patterns.

Another Abenaki skill, basketry, became an important part of their culture and also of their economy. Splint-basket making, the weaving of strips or splints of wood, became widespread in the Northeast after Europeans introduced the metal tools needed to cut the thin strips of wood used to make the basket. Ash is an ideal wood for this technique because it is both strong and pliable. Abenaki men usually prepared the splints and women plaited them, often interweaving twisted or braided sweet grass. In the late 19th and early 20th centuries, Abenaki living in St. Francis, Quebec, peddled splint baskets to tourists and to suppliers who furnished the goods to stores in Montreal and Quebec. Penobscot basketmakers on Indian Island at Old Town, Maine, also became well known for their art. Today, however, only a few basketmakers keep the art alive, and unless more young people take an interest in learning and preserving it, the craft may soon die out.

Other materials used by the Abenaki to decorate household wares include paint, shells, and quills. Shell beads—known as wampum—were

Two decorative birchbark boxes. The larger one, from Quebec, is trimmed with sweetgrass and is decorated with "positive etching," the scratching of a dark pattern on a light background. The smaller box, from Maine, features "negative etching," a light pattern on a dark background.

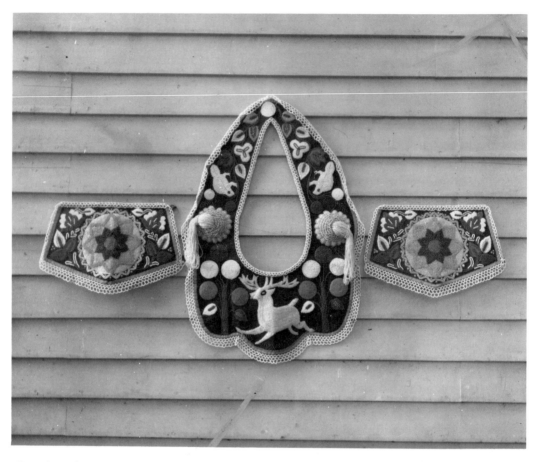

Once introduced to such European goods as broadcloth, the Abenaki devised new designs for their traditional clothing. The ceremonial collar and cuffs shown here are decorated with hand-sewn flowers, beaver, and moose.

strung on leather thongs and in early times were used as a kind of currency as well as in ceremonies and treaty negotiations. Sometimes Abenaki wove the strings into belts or combined white and purple shells to decorate belts, necklaces, collars, and capes with attractive designs. In 1700, the Abenaki sent a beautiful, six-foot-long wampum belt to Chartres Cathedral in France, where it is still on display. After European traders arrived in North America, the Abenaki also began to use glass beads. These were brightly colored and were easier to work into intricate designs than the shells.

Before the arrival of Europeans, the Abenaki decorated clothes made of moose- or deerskin with paint, porcupine quills, shells, and moose hair.

After European contact, they took to wearing cloth instead of hides and decorated their robes with glass beads and ribbons. After Penobscot artists began to obtain red and black broadcloth from traders or from the government as part of their treaty agreements, they developed a reputation for making beautiful coats of the material, embroidering it with white beadwork and ribbon appliqué. A chief's coat decorated in this way was both a mark of prestige and a work of art. Beads found their way onto caps, shirts, skirts, moccasins, belts, and hair ornaments. Abenaki sometimes took silver coins to a colonial silversmith who fashioned them into ornaments using traditional designs; they wore these brooches to adorn their finest outfits.

The wide diversity of Abenaki art maintained certain common designs, some of which may once have had spiritual meanings. Favorite motifs included zigzags and triangles. Crosses became popular after the introduction of Christianity. The most popular design of all was the double-curve pattern, which Abenaki artists used mostly as a foundation for their designs, embellishing it with a variety of floral and geometric patterns. The double-curve pattern carries the visible suggestion of flowers, plants, and leaves; it may also symbolize the relationship between the chiefs and the people and unity between bands.

Abenaki song, clothing, beadwork, and basketry all changed in the years following initial contact with Europeans. Yet Abenaki art survived as a means of expression for the people's tastes, traditions, beliefs, and values. Remarkably, much Abenaki culture and art have been maintained in the face of the tremendous upheavals in their world caused by the European invasion of America. ▲

This Catholic church at Odanak, Quebec, the town's fourth, was built in 1900 by Abenaki whose forebears were converted to Christianity by French Jesuit missionaries.

TRADERS, DISEASES, AND MISSIONARIES

The Abenaki of Maine were among the first Indians in North America to meet Europeans. In fact, they grew accustomed to having white men on their shores long before the Pilgrims landed at Plymouth Rock. About 1,000 years ago, the people who lived in the Dawnland may have heard rumors that strange white men had been glimpsed in lands far to the north. Viking seafarers, pushing west in their dragon-headed longboats, visited Greenland and Newfoundland almost 500 years before Christopher Columbus reached the New World. The Vikings probably did not venture as far south as Maine, but in the next two centuries the Abenaki did see increasing numbers of European sailors, voyaging in huge boats propelled by giant white sails. These strangers behaved in ways that the Abenaki regarded as rude and odd. They also spoke harsh-sounding languages and brought with them goods new to the Abenaki.

These first Europeans were few in number and posed no evident threat to the Abenaki. The Abenaki sometimes traded with them, exchanging furs and foods for the Europeans' cloth and metal. They had no reason to suspect that the newcomers also carried with them the seeds of destruction. Before long, the Abenaki would have to fight to defend their lands and culture against a new wave of Europeans—English farmers and soldiers. And, beginning in the late 16th century and throughout the 17th century, the greatest danger to the Abenaki came not from armies of men but from European diseases, manufactured goods, and missionary Christians.

English, Scandinavian, Spanish, and French fishermen first skirted the coast of Maine in the late 1400s, returning home with large catches of cod. Columbus's well-known voyage in 1492 and the spectacular success of the Spaniards in conquering the Aztec empire of Mexico inspired more and more Europeans to venture west in search of riches. Rumors of a fabulously rich city called Norumbega lured many adventurers to Maine. Norumbega did not exist except in the imaginations of

41

adventurers and empire builders. But the foreigners kept coming.

Giovanni da Verrazano, a Florentine sailing in the service of the French Crown, traveled along the Maine coast in 1524 and left one of the earliest written descriptions of the Abenaki. He found that the Abenaki had already had some experience dealing with Europeans and were extremely wary. They treated Verrazano's men with contempt and agreed to trade only by lowering a basket from the rocks to the Europeans'

The gravestone of Martin Pring, an English explorer who traveled along the Maine coastline in 1604.

boat as it bobbed in the waves. When Verrazano led a landing party ashore, the Abenaki fired a hail of arrows to let the Europeans know they were not welcome. Verrazano went away convinced they were "bad people."

A year later a Spaniard, Esteban Gómez, explored Penobscot Bay, as did Simón Ferdinando, a Portuguese navigator working for England, in 1579. The next year, Englishman John Walker visited the region in the hope of locating Norumbega and establishing a colony there. In 1583, Frenchman Étienne Bellenger traded with the Indians of Maine for furs. English navigator Bartholomew Gosnold sailed down the southern coast of Maine in 1602, and in 1604 another Englishman, Martin Pring, sailed into Casco Bay, trading for furs with the Indians along the coast. The French explorer Samuel de Champlain visited Abenaki villages as he edged along the coast between Saco Bay and the St. John River in 1604 and 1605 and left further accounts of the Indian inhabitants. The Abenaki were being pulled into increasing contact with Europe, but they had as yet no real cause for alarm.

Then, in 1605, Captain George Waymouth touched off the first of many unfriendly incidents between the English and the Abenaki. The English sea captain abducted five Abenaki and sailed home with them as captives. In England, Sir Ferdinando Gorges and George Popham, two other explorers working for King James I, questioned the captives closely about their lands and decided that a permanent colony could be established in Abenaki country. One of the captives, a man named Nahanda, returned home in 1606. In 1607, a second captive, Skidwaros, returned as a reluctant guide for George Popham and a group of settlers who planned to establish a colony on the Kennebec River. Meanwhile, Nahanda had warned his people about the English, and the Abenaki were wary of the intruders—relations were cold and unfriendly. The English established Popham Colony at Sagadahoc, but the winter of 1607–08 was long and hard. When Popham died, the colony was abandoned.

The French, too, attempted to colonize Abenaki land. They built a mission and colony called St. Saveur on Mount Desert Island, but it was destroyed in 1613 by the English, who still hoped to establish a permanent English settlement in Maine. Gorges pinned his hopes on Captain John Smith, the founder and hero of Jamestown Colony in Virginia, who led the next venture. Smith reached Penobscot Bay in 1614. On a later voyage he was captured by the French but not before he wrote *A Description of New England* (1616), in which he reported his thoughts on the area. Smith never gave up his dreams of establishing a colony.

Another Englishman who shared Smith's vision was Christopher Levett. He sailed along the Maine coast in 1623–24, traded with the Abenaki, and tried to establish a colony at Casco Bay.

In the early 1600s, Samuel de Champlain became the first French explorer to reach the Abenaki homelands. The lake named for him marked the western border of Abenaki soil and now serves as part of the Vermont–New York border.

He, too, left written descriptions of Maine's coast, but like his predecessors, he failed to establish a permanent settlement in the rugged north woods. He died at sea in 1630.

The English persevered as their maps and sailing ships improved and

Point Popham, Maine, in 1891, almost 300 years after the English established their first colony in Abenaki territory there. That early settlement—at a place the Indians called Sagadahoc—failed after a severe winter.

as colonies in Virginia and Massachusetts took root. King Charles I granted Sir Ferdinando Gorges extensive lands in Maine and in 1637 appointed him governor of all New England. But the English Civil War in the 1640s—which pitted Puritan Oliver Cromwell against those loyal to Charles—disrupted Gorges's plans, and he, too, died without ever seeing his dreams of settlement realized. By the middle of the 17th century, the French claimed to control much of the territory east of the Penobscot River, and the Puritan English who were established in Massachusetts Bay cast covetous eyes northward to Abenaki country. In reality, however, the Abenaki remained in control.

Eventually, the Abenakis' location—midway between rival French and English colonists—dictated the course of their history, but in the 17th century they were more affected by something else: disease. The first Europeans brought with them germs and viruses that American Indians had never encountered before. Indians died by the thousands of smallpox, bubonic plague, measles, yellow fever, influenza, and other ailments.

The most devastating epidemic in New England was a massive outbreak of either smallpox or plague (historians are still divided) that raged among the tribes from 1616 to 1619. Many villages were totally destroyed and whole populations were swept away. The survivors fled their homes, abandoning their fields and leaving wigwams filled with corpses. The disease reached the Abenaki in 1617 and sped along the coast of Maine. In some areas, more than 75 percent of the Indians were probably wiped out.

Another huge epidemic—smallpox—struck in 1633–34. It swept along the St. Lawrence Valley, down the Connecticut River, and through New England. The death rate was appalling. William Bradford, the governor of Plymouth Colony, reported that in one Indian village up the Connecticut River 950 Indians perished out of a population of 1,000, "and many did rott above ground for want of burial."

Smallpox hit the Abenaki again in 1639, and seven years later, large numbers of them died from a disease that caused its victims to vomit blood. Smaller epidemics and infection by other diseases continued to kill Abenaki throughout the century. One writer has suggested that recurrent outbreaks of disease reduced the population of western Abenaki in Vermont and New Hampshire from as many as 10,000 to as few as 500.

The impact of disease on the Abenaki cannot be measured only in terms of fatalities. Survivors who had seen their friends and relatives die a horrible

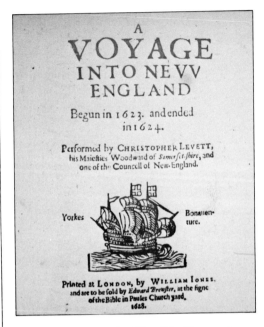

Knowledge about the New World spread rapidly in London, England, through such accounts as Christopher Levett's A Voyage into New England, *published in 1628.*

death often experienced psychological trauma. Family bands that had lost many of their key members struggled to survive. Diseases disrupted traditional patterns of hunting, fishing, and planting and disturbed the people's social and ceremonial life. By the time English soldiers and settlers began to invade their lands, the Abenaki had already suffered great losses from the viral invasion.

European fur traders brought more turmoil to the Abenaki world. Bands had traded with other Indians long before Europeans arrived, and they soon took to trading with the newcomers. In doing so, they opened up their world to dramatic and often deadly changes. European traders carried diseases, as did their goods, which were often infected from being handled. The presence of the traders provoked further rivalry between different Indian tribes (for the right to supply furs to the Europeans) and led to changes in Indian warfare and ways of life.

The Abenaki on the coast of Maine traded with Europeans early in the 16th century. Before long, beaver hats became fashionable in Europe, and the fur trade grew into a profitable business. As European rivals began to compete for the Indians' trade, the Abenaki found themselves wooed by the French in Canada as well as by merchants in New England. The English and French built trading posts at key locations in the hope of attracting Indian hunters who might otherwise travel to do business with their rivals. By the early 17th century, trading posts stood along the Piscataqua and Kennebec rivers, as well as at Casco Bay and Pemaquid, in Maine. By mid-century, trading posts on the Merrimack and Connecticut rivers, farther to the north and west, gave whites their first regular contact with the western Abenaki.

The fur trade could not continue without the Indians, and the Abenaki took what they needed from it. Although they continued to use items made from stone, shell, and bone, they came to rely on traders for weapons, tools, and jewelry. European metal, in particular, proved a boon because it could improve the quality of traditional Abenaki implements. The new tools enabled farmers to cultivate more corn, artisans to carve with greater precision, and hunters to make better snowshoes, bows, canoes, and paddles. Abenaki ornaments now included brass, and cloth obtained from traders could be made into Abenaki-style garments and decorated with glass beads and ribbons.

Yet the fur trade proved a mixed blessing for the Abenaki. As early as 1607, competition for access to European trade pitted eastern Abenaki against neighboring Micmac bands. In later years, Iroquois raids from the west put the Abenaki under growing pressure. Not only did the fur trade escalate tribal warfare; it also made warfare more deadly. In the days before European traders sold them guns, Indians had fought with weapons made of wood and stone and had battled on a small scale, usually to seek revenge and prestige and occasionally to defend their boundaries. These skirmishes caused few casualties. Now Indian war parties, armed with guns, clashed against each other more often and with more lethal consequences.

Colonial authorities tried to limit the gun trade, but the Abenaki had been in possession of firearms as early as 1637 and since then had been caught up in the deadly cycle of competition for furs and firearms—they needed furs to trade for guns and needed guns to fight for control of trade routes and hunting territories. The Abenaki, in short, devoted more energy to war and spent more time hunting. Before long, they disrupted the sacred relationship that had traditionally existed between the hunter and the animal world.

At the same time, traders introduced alcohol to the Abenaki—with disastrous results. Missionaries and colonial authorities complained that alcohol had an evil effect on the Abenaki. Drunkenness led to quarrels, discord, and murders and placed new strains on Abenaki communities, which had always valued harmony. Some families went hungry as hunters bartered their furs for a bottle at the trading post. But traders knew the steady sale of whiskey guaranteed good profits, and so they continued to sell it.

While the Abenaki reeled under the impact of these new forces, European missionaries came to their villages preaching alien religious beliefs. Europe at that time was bitterly divided between Catholicism and Protestant-

As the Abenaki came into greater contact wih European traders, they incorporated new materials into their tools. The blades on these knives are made of metal rather than bone, as had been their practice for centuries.

The influence of Christianity is evident on this carving done by an Abenaki in Odanak, Quebec. The Virgin Mary (center) is flanked by animals and the sun. (The Abenaki did not make totem poles as such; that term applies only to carvings done in the Pacific Northwest.)

ism, and Europeans in North America competed for the Indians' souls as well as for their trade and allegiance. Black-robed Jesuit missionaries traveled the length of New France (Canada) and into northern New England to carry Catholicism to the Indians living there. The French built a mission on the Kennebec River in 1646, and missionaries were active in Abenaki villages throughout Maine. In later years, mission villages grew up at Cowass on the upper Connecticut River and on Lake Champlain, as well as at St. Francis, Sillery, and Becancour on the banks of the St. Lawrence. Many Abenaki and Sokoki from the south visited these Canadian missions; others took refuge there in times of war against the English.

The English tried to counteract French influence by sending their own, Protestant, ministers to convert the Abenaki, but with little luck. The tenacious piety of the Jesuits—a Catholic order—combined with the English Puritans' reputation (among the Indians) for cruelty and treachery led the Abenaki to favor the French.

Within Abenaki villages, Jesuit missionaries contested local shamans for spiritual leadership. The missionaries tried to undermine the shamans' authority, especially after the shamans proved unable to protect their people from the new diseases spread by the Europeans. Some Abenaki turned to the French missionaries in times of crisis. The missionaries, for their part, took every opportunity to point up the failure of the shamans.

French priests baptized, married, and buried many Abenaki and otherwise carried out the practices of the Catholic faith. Indeed, the oldest Catholic cemetery in New England is on Indian Island, Maine; it dates from 1688. Catholic churches became a central feature in many Abenaki villages, and Catholic priests and nuns became prominent leaders and teachers in many communities well into the 20th century.

Jesuit priests hoped Indian converts would completely abandon their old beliefs, and they looked for evidence that this momentous conversion had occurred. Early in the 18th century, Father Sebastian Rasles declared that "the whole Abenaki Nation is Christian and is very zealous in preserving its Religion." But the matter was not so easily decided. Abenaki who adopted Christianity did not necessarily toss aside their traditional beliefs; often they accepted only the outward forms of Christianity or simply grafted elements of the new teachings onto their old religion. And, as the French Jesuit Father Jean Enjarlan found at Sillery, there were always some Abenaki who were "still rebellious to the light."

Nevertheless, from the 17th century on, French priests and the Catholic religion exerted a tremendous influence on Abenaki society. Among the more evident examples of this legacy are the many modern Abenaki names derived from French names first given to the tribe by missionaries during baptism: Attean, for instance, came from the French Étienne, or Steven; Sabadis is an abridgment of Saint Jean-Baptist. More than the Abenaki's culture, though, was changed. Because they were aligned in some ways with the French Catholics against the English Protestants, the tribe's very future would also be affected.

During the first two centuries of European presence in the Dawnland, the Abenaki faced powerful new forces that disrupted their old ways of life and drained their strength. They preserved their culture by adjusting to new circumstances and incorporating new elements. Their communities proved to be extremely adaptable and resilient. Despite serious losses, the Abenaki still presented a formidable threat to the English soldiers and settlers who invaded their territory on the heels of epidemics, fur traders, and missionaries. ▲

Joe Francis, sagamore of the Penobscot, at Indian Island, Maine, in about 1900. Despite the disruption their way of life suffered as a result of war, disease, and migration, the Abenaki maintained much of their traditional dress and tribal organization.

WARS
AND
MIGRATIONS

In the 18th century the Abenaki earned a reputation as fierce warriors and merciless enemies. Generations of writers portrayed them as the shock troops of the French in Canada and the scourge of the New England frontier. From the 1670s to the 1760s the Abenaki fought five wars against the English in an effort to stave off the invasion of their homeland, and they frequently helped the French in their conflicts with the English. The Abenaki won many victories, but relentless pressure from the English pushed them back, and their French allies let them down. Between about 1650 and 1800, many Abenaki migrated from their original homelands to seek safer locations in far northern New England and in Canada.

Europeans did not introduce warfare to the Indians, of course. Tribes had been battling for hundreds of years. Still, Indians spent more time fighting after European contact than before it. And the Abenaki had little choice but to become warlike if they were to survive in a world of many enemies.

The most belligerent tribe in the northeast was the Iroquois of New York, who began to wage war on neighboring tribes in the 17th century. Armed with guns and prodded by the demand for furs, Iroquois war parties traveled far and wide, reaching into Canada and across Lake Champlain into Abenaki country. The Sokoki and Abenaki held their own against the raiders, but in December 1663 the Iroquois laid siege to the Sokoki village at Fort Hill, overlooking the Connecticut River in New Hampshire. The Sokoki staved off the attackers but were forced to evacuate their village. Some fled to live among their neighbors; others remained only in small bands that hid from general view. Further Iroquois campaigns followed, with war parties penetrating deep into Abenaki territory. The Abenaki retaliated by staging their own raids against the Iroquois, and Abenaki warriors joined French soldiers who marched with fire and sword into the heart of Iroquois territory. Some Sokoki retreated to Canada in the 1660s to escape the warfare.

51

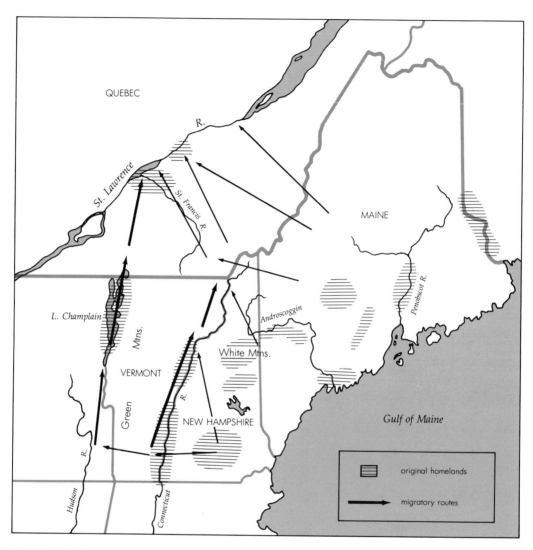

More lethal than the Iroquois—and a faster-growing threat—were the English. Word of their military prowess probably reached the Abenaki in 1637, when an army of English Puritans destroyed the main village of the Pequot Indians on the Mystic River in Connecticut. They burned the Indians'

homes, killed men, women, and children, and sent the survivors fleeing for cover. Appalled by the brutal manner of English warfare, the Abenaki fixed their attention on these enemies, who were advancing from the south.

Tensions mounted as English settlers pushed into Indian lands. The sachem (leader) Massasoit—of the Wampanoag Indians in Massachusetts—kept an uneasy truce with the English, but when he died in 1661 and his son Metacom became sachem, the peace eroded. In 1675 a major war broke out across southern New England when Metacom (whom the English called King Philip) led an army made up of several tribes. The Abenaki joined the fight after English sailors on the Saco River drowned the baby son of Squando, one of their chiefs. At first, the Indians proved successful—of the 90 white settlements in Indian homelands, 52 were attacked and 12 were completely wiped out. But Metacom, who did not command the wide respect that his father had, faced trouble in keeping together his coalition of New England tribes. Some Indians defected to the other side, and the war turned brutal and bloody. The English suffered heavy losses before the Indians were finally defeated and Metacom was killed in 1676. An Abenaki chief called Mogg signed a peace treaty with the English in that year, but sporadic fighting between the Abenaki and the English continued for many months after the so-called King Philip's War ended in the south.

The defeat threw the New England tribes into disarray. Indian refugees from southern New England traveled north, looking for safety in Abenaki country, and many Abenaki also retreated to more remote locations. Many Sokoki and Abenaki migrated to mission villages in Canada. The French welcomed the refugees with open arms and gave them food, protection, and advice: They never failed to remind the Indians that they should suspect the English of intending to destroy them and take their lands. These suspicions proved valid.

Whereas the Puritan English looked on the Abenaki as "savage heathens" and waged ruthless war against them, the French sent traders and missionaries into the Indians' villages to live with the Abenaki and win their friendship. One such trader was the Baron de St. Castine, who came to the town of Pentaguoet on the Penobscot River in 1670 and married the daughter of chief Madockawando. When Anglo-French rivalry in Europe spilled over into war in North America, the Abenaki found themselves caught in the middle. They rarely had any doubt, however, about which side to support.

The European part of the clash was called the War of the League of Augsburg; its American counterpart was King William's War (1689–98), named for William II, king of England. In 1690, Governor Louis Frontenac of New France dispatched three expeditions from the north, striking the English towns of Schenectady, New York; Salmon Falls, New Hampshire; and Casco Bay, Maine. Abenaki warriors took part in these raids, as well as in raids on the Maine towns of Pemaquid, Berwick, North Yarmouth, and Oyster River. The English retaliated with

In 1670, Baron de Castine, a French trader, married the daughter of an Abenaki chief. The French were generally less hostile than the English toward American Indians.

strikes of their own, destroying Castine's post at Pentaguoet. The Connecticut and Champlain valleys became thoroughfares for war parties, and those Sokoki who had drifted back to their homes in the middle reaches of the Connecticut River after King Philip's War moved out of harm's way. Other Abenaki sought refuge from the war by moving closer to their French allies in Canada.

Only a brief lull in hostilities followed King William's War before the outbreak of Queen Anne's War (known in Europe as the War of the Spanish Succession) in 1702. Again, the French and Abenaki took the offensive, launching attacks on the Maine towns of Wells, Portland, and Scarborough. Abenaki warriors participated in the raid on Deerfield, Massachusetts, in February 1704 in which a large force of French and Indians traveling on snowshoes surprised the sleeping town at dawn, torched most of its buildings, and escaped up the frozen Connecticut River with more than 100 captives.

The Abenaki regularly took captives during the era of frontier wars. Sometimes they sold them to the French for ransom, but they also adopted individuals into their own bands as replacements for members who had died. Some of these captives came to prefer their new existence. Those who had been captured as children grew up thinking of themselves as Abenaki, later raising their own Abenaki families. This melding together of two cultures is still evident. Several prominent modern-day Abenaki family names can be traced back to English captives taken during these wars.

Fearsome though the New England Indians proved in their raids, the military power they could muster on their own was waning—too many young Indians were dying, and the supply of European soldiers seemed limitless. The English, for their part, were re-

lentless. They responded to raids by of-
fering bounties for Abenaki scalps and
sending expeditions to search out and
destroy Abenaki villages. Many Abenaki accepted French offers of protection
and moved to Canada. An Abenaki
mission village was founded at Becancour, on the St. Lawrence River,
in 1704. Others simply melted into the
forests as their enemies approached.
English soldiers often came upon completely deserted villages. Such tactics
helped the Abenaki to limit their losses.

The tribe suffered defeat of a different kind under the Treaty of Utrecht,
which was negotiated in the Nether-
lands in 1713. French negotiators at the
peace talks agreed to hand over a great
deal of territory to the English, including Acadia (the present areas of Nova
Scotia, New Brunswick, and part of
northern Maine), which contained
much Abenaki land. The Abenaki did
not consider themselves defeated in
battle, and many felt betrayed by the
French negotiators in Europe.

England and France maintained a
hostile peace for 30 years after the
Treaty of Utrecht, but the Abenaki were
at war with the English again in the
1720s. In this era, they fought for their
own reasons, with or without French
backing. The English were trespassing
and building forts on lands more than
100 miles northeast of their first villages, and when Abenaki complaints
about this further encroachment were
ignored, war broke out again. Known
generally as Dummer's War or Love-

In 1690, Governor Louis Frontenac of New France (Canada) sent raiding parties, which included Abenaki warriors, to assault English towns in northern New England.

well's War (named for Captain John
Lovewell), the conflict caused serious
losses on both sides. In 1723, English
troops burned the deserted Penobscot
village at Old Town, Maine. The following year, Captain Jeremiah Moulton
and a force of soldiers destroyed the

village of Norridgewock and killed and scalped the resident French priest, Father Sebastian Rasles, who had lived among the Abenaki for some 30 years. Abenaki tradition, supported in part by an unfinished letter by Father Rasles, relates that a shaman foretold the attack on Norridgewock in time for the people to flee, but only a few made their escape before the soldiers arrived. Many refugees from Norridgewock fled to Old Town in Penobscot country.

In 1725, Captain Lovewell fought a costly battle with the Pigwacket at the head of the Saco River, near Fryeburg, Maine. Both he and Paugus, an Indian chief, perished in the conflict. Many

Penobscot, as well as disheartened Pigwacket and refugees from Norridgewock, made the trek north toward the French mission villages or other safer sites before the war ended in 1727.

In Vermont, Abenaki from Lake Champlain fought their own war against the northern and western frontier settlements of Massachusetts. Chief Grey Lock, himself a refugee from his homeland in Massachusetts, rallied western Abenaki and other displaced warriors at Grey Lock's Castle near Missisquoi. From there they launched lightning raids south through the Green Mountains, striking the English almost at will. The English could neither defeat

This lithograph shows the death of Father Sebastian Rasles, a French missionary who lived for 30 years among the Abenaki. He was scalped by the English in a 1724 raid.

In a rare tribute to Indians, the English named this peak in Massachusetts's Berkshire Hills for Chief Grey Lock, who led the Missisquoi in defiant raids on English towns after most other Abenaki had been subdued.

Grey Lock nor bring him to the peace table, and he remained defiant even after the eastern Abenaki had made peace. Later, the descendants of Grey Lock's enemies named a peak in the Berkshire Hills of Massachusetts in the chief's honor.

The Abenaki enjoyed peace from 1727 until 1744, when Anglo-French hostilities flared up again. Even during this brief calm, however, the English continued to threaten Abenaki land. Colonial farmers edged up the Connecticut and Merrimack valleys, and by 1742 some 12,000 settlers lived in Maine. Not surprisingly, when King George's War broke out, the Abenaki joined the French once again in trying to stem this English tide. Warriors from Missisquoi, St. Francis, and Becancour joined French campaigns or headed out in small parties to harass the English on the frontier. English settlers in the Connecticut Valley abandoned their farms and fields as small garrison forts proved incapable of protecting them against the "French and Indian menace."

This "menace" was ended for good by the Seven Years' War (1756–63), called in America the French and Indian War. Britain defeated France and Spain, among others, ending their colonial

During the siege of Quebec, in 1759, the French army of General Louis Montcalm (on horse), which included some Abenaki fighters, fell to the English, led by Major General James Wolfe (with sword). The English then took control of Canada.

presence in eastern North America. During the conflict, some Abenaki warriors served the French as scouts and conducted their own raids as soldiers. They fought at the Battle of Monongahela, in Pennsylvania, at which the French and their Indian allies routed the English army under General Braddock. The Abenaki also participated in the capture of Fort Oswego and Fort William Henry, in New York, and served with General Louis Montcalm's army at the siege of Quebec.

But English military and naval power gradually pushed the French to the brink of defeat. In 1759, Major Robert Rogers and a force of infantry, the so-called Rangers—who were trained in Indian fighting—attacked and destroyed the Abenaki village at St. Francis. They burned its chapel and homes and destroyed the mission's records.

The Abenaki called Rogers *Wobi Madaondo*—the White Devil. Rogers claimed that 200 Abenaki died in the attacks—clearly an exaggeration. The Abenaki managed to inflict casualties on the English as they made their way home. (A fictionalized and biased account of Rogers's raid is provided in Kenneth Roberts's 1936 novel *Northwest Passage*, made into a movie in 1940. The book and movie both helped perpetuate the image of the Abenaki as bloodthirsty savages.)

The Abenaki suffered a more permanent blow when, after half a century of conflict in North America, the English defeated the French on all fronts and took possession of Canada. At the end of a long war, the Abenaki found they were now expected to answer to King George III of England rather than deal as allies with King Louis XV of France.

The Kennebec, Penobscot, and Passamaquoddy remained in their original locations, but other Abenaki bands scattered in the wake of war and conquest. Some took refuge among the Mohawk at St. Regis, New York, or in other Iroquois communities. Many made their way to the village at St. Francis, and for this reason the English often referred to all Abenaki in Canada and Vermont as "St. Francis Indians," as if they were a distinct tribe. In fact, the St. Francis Indians were Sokoki and Abenaki refugees whose life had been disrupted in the era of recurrent warfare. Perhaps no more than 1,000 Abenaki survived in Maine at the end of the war. Generations of warfare against the English, combined with cold, hunger, and disease, had reduced the Abenaki to a shadow of their former strength.

The conquest of Canada opened northern New England to a flood of English settlers. Without a French presence in the area, the Abenaki were left to face this flood alone. English farmers settled in Maine, Vermont, and New Hampshire in greater numbers than the

Major Robert Rogers of the British Army showed little mercy to Indians who aided the French. In 1759 his infantry burned the Abenaki village at St. Francis, Quebec, including its church. The refugee Abenaki living there called Rogers "the White Devil."

Abenaki had ever seen, and they over-ran lands that the Abenaki had once hunted and planted and fought courageously to defend. Those Abenaki who remained in their homelands found themselves pushed onto less productive land. There was little they could do.

Another violent phase of Abenaki history began in 1776, when the American Revolution erupted. Some of the Abenaki in Canada sided with the British redcoats, and Indians from St. Francis and Becancour served as scouts for them. But many Abenaki pitched in to help the rebel colonists. Because the Americans needed their help—the Indians inhabited a strategically important region—the Massachusetts

provincial congress took steps to prevent settlers from trespassing on the lands of their Penobscot "brethren," and General George Washington sent a pledge of friendship to the Passamaquoddy.

The Penobscot chief Joseph Orono and Francis Joseph Neptune of the Passamaquoddy led their people in support of the Americans and helped turn back British attacks in eastern Maine. In 1777, the Passamaquoddy aided the colonists at a crucial juncture of the conflict, when they fended off a British naval expedition at Machias, Maine. In 1780, Orono and several other chiefs visited Boston, Massachusetts, and Newport, Rhode Island, where they

A Penobscot ferryman approaches Indian Island, Maine, about 1910.

This plaque records the tercentenary of St. Francis, Quebec (now called Odanak), in English, French, and Abenaki.

were entertained by the officers and shown the French warships that had been sent to help the Americans. Orono carved on his hunting horn the things he saw during his trip.

In 1783, England signed the Peace of Paris, which recognized the independence of the 13 American colonies and also established a border between the new United States and the British territory of Canada. For the first time, a political boundary separated the Abenaki at St. Francis and other Canadian villages from their relatives to the south. Abenaki continued to travel across the border, but as Orono and Francis Joseph Neptune clearly recognized, their brethren who remained in the United States would have to come to terms with the new nation. Joseph Orono died in 1801. The town of Orono, Maine, was later named for him.

In the difficult years that followed, the Abenaki of Maine and Vermont struggled both to get along with the Americans who had taken over most of their lands and to deal with the federal and state governments. It seemed unlikely that they could survive in the new nation without losing their own political and cultural identity. ▲

Molly Molasses, a Penobscot elder, wearing an elaborately embroidered conical cap and two large medallions.

THE
SURVIVAL
OF THE
PEOPLE

The American Revolution ended in 1783 with the colonists winning their independence. But it did not help the Abenaki, who had been fighting for their own independence for more than 150 years. The generations of warfare and forced migration were over, but a new crisis greeted the Abenaki in Maine, Vermont, New Hampshire, and Quebec. They struggled to keep their lands, to control their own affairs, and to preserve their culture and identity in the face of overwhelming odds. The 1800s were dark years for the Abenaki, and at times the people seemed in danger of losing everything they held dear. Yet through this period of hardship and struggle, they preserved the strength and values that would allow them to reassert themselves in later years.

Many Abenaki had migrated to Canada during the wars of the 18th century, making new homes in Quebec, especially in St. Francis and Becancour, which became major centers of the Abenaki population. In fact, so many Abenaki flooded into St. Francis following the revolutionary war that in 1805 the English Crown allotted the Abenaki new homesteads in the Durham Reserve in Quebec.

Those Abenaki who chose to remain in the United States and tried to hold on to their ancestral homelands had a hard climb ahead of them. Not only did settlers and speculators continue to encroach on their lands, but the Abenaki also had to deal with the federal and state governments, who offered little or no protection and seemed to expect that the Abenaki would give up their ancestral ways.

The main threat, however, came from settlers, who invaded Abenaki country in growing numbers. It mattered little to them that the Penobscot and Passamaquoddy had never abandoned their lands during the French and Indian Wars and had helped the Americans during the Revolution. To

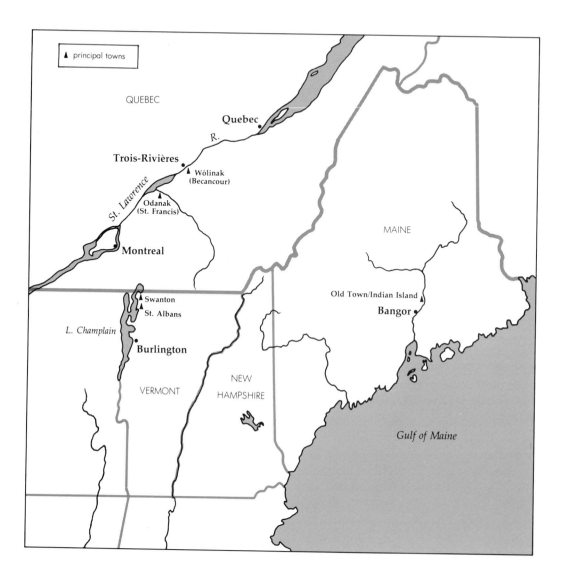

the white pioneers, the Abenaki were a defeated people with no claims to the land they inhabited.

In Vermont, the western Abenaki who remained around the north end of Lake Champlain fared little better. Land speculators such as Ira and Ethan Allen secured possession of their lands, and settlers edged them into remote marginal areas. The white population rose steadily, forcing the Abenaki to abandon their village at Missisquoi. Some joined their relatives across the border at St. Francis; others continued to live in the surrounding country, where they traveled in small family bands and

(continued on page 73)

FROM FOREST, LAKE, AND LAND

The Abenaki use ash splints to make everything from pincushions to fancy baskets; this knitting basket incorporates woven sweet grass as well. The hole on top is for yarn and needles.

Abenaki crafts served a dual purpose: They added beauty to daily life and paid tribute to the cycle of nature's harmony that informed the people's deepest beliefs. Thus, for thousands of years, Abenaki craftworkers used natural materials to create functional and decorative items. From the wood and bark of the birch tree, they fashioned canoes and boxes; from plaited splints of ash wood, they made beautiful and unusual baskets. Men carved bone into knife blades; women strung shells into bracelets and necklaces. And children played with toys that everyone made from a wealth of materials.

A regular routine for women was tanning moose, deer, and beaver skins into durable hide ideal for shirts, dresses, and shoes, all of them sewn with needles made from porcupine quills. These items and others were often enlivened with colored dyes extracted from berries and plants.

Once Europeans arrived on their lands, the "people of the Dawnland" began to modify their crafts. Wool cloth, metal tools, and glass beads were foremost among the trade goods that broadened the range of the artists' creativity.

Today the Abenaki build fewer canoes and hone fewer knives than they once did, and their artful baskets are made for the tourist market. Nevertheless, Abenaki crafts retain a high level of artistry and continue to incorporate the rich themes—the legends, myths, and symbols—that make their culture so distinct. Materials and designs alike still bespeak a natural balance between humans and their creator. And the majesty of the "Dawnland" is still reflected in Abenaki art.

Braided sweet grass can be used decoratively—for trim—as well as functionally. The tallest of these contemporary baskets is 11 ½ inches high.

Many contemporary Penobscot baskets feature multi-colored bands and such intricate elements as the turned-out loops shown here.

Abenaki lidded baskets of the mid-19th century came in a great variety of styles; this 1885 Penobscot piece holds sewing materials. Its ash-splint bands were probably once dyed a deep indigo, now somewhat faded.

This 19th-century Passamaquoddy belt depicts the traditional wigwams and trees. (A third wigwam beginning at right indicates the piece was once broken.) Wampum—embroidered strands of tubular quahog-shell beads—is one of the oldest Abenaki crafts.

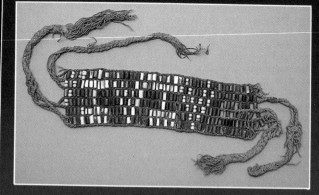

Tomah Joseph, a Passamaquoddy artist who worked until 1914, near Perry, Maine, was also a canoe guide, book illustrator, tribal governor, story-teller, and craftsman. He made this birchbark etching on the back of a pic-ture frame. Its three panels tell a story from what Tomah called the "old days": Hunters pursue a deer (in winter—note the snowshoes), they capture

ber of birchbark boxes for the tourist market—to hold jewelry, gloves, trinkets, or to stand on their own as works of art. The words *Kolele Mooke* on the smallest box, which held playing cards, mean "Have good luck." But few tourists understood his language.

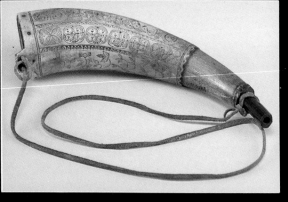

Horns for carrying gunpowder were introduced to the Abenaki by European soldiers. This 19th-century cattle horn is incised with drawings by a Penobscot.

A knife made strictly for ornamental purposes. Its carved handle is adorned with a beaver, facing away from the blade.

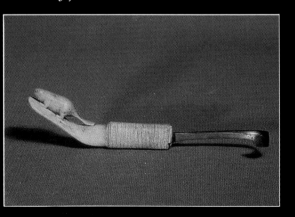

Senabeh Francis of the Penobscot carved and painted this ceremonial war club. What were once

(continued from page 64)

camped, hunted, and fished in familiar places. The Abenaki in the area of Swanton, Highgate, and St. Albans, Vermont, kept a low profile in the hope of avoiding attention and hostility. Americans who saw them assumed they were merely wandering Indians from Canada who did not "belong" in the United States.

Even as the Abenaki adjusted to new circumstances and tried to retain old values, the Dawnland world changed before their eyes. The fur trade that had been an important part of the Abenaki economy for two centuries was dying out because large-scale hunting and trapping had killed off huge numbers of beaver. Prime game, such as caribou and moose, was becoming rare. Farmers and lumberers cut into the forests of northern New England. In 1825 the Great Miramichi Fire raged across much of New Brunswick and Maine, burning timberland, killing off wildlife, and destroying the Penobscot village at Mattawamkeag. Throughout the period, cholera and other diseases thinned the Abenaki population.

After the American Revolution, the fur trade died out and lumbering became the greatest threat to Abenaki lands, as thousands of oaks such as this one were felled. Those Indians who had not died in wars or from disease either kept a low profile or moved to Quebec.

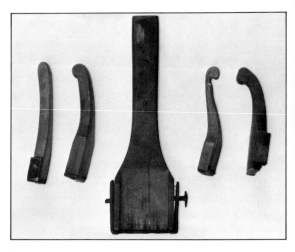

Left: *Basket making became a chief source of income for many New England Indians who could no longer hunt their old lands.*
Above: *Cutters made of wood and metal were used to prepare the ash splints for baskets.*

As Americans took control over the best lands, many Abenaki found they could no longer support themselves in the old way by hunting, fishing, and planting. In the face of a declining fur trade, the Abenaki began to supplement their income by making baskets, moccasins, snowshoes, canoes, and paddles and selling these goods in local white communities.

In time, Abenaki from St. Francis found they could earn good money by traveling to tourist resorts in the northern United States and selling splint-ash baskets. Originally made for the Abenaki themselves to store and carry food and fruit, these baskets now were made chiefly for tourists. But by the late 19th century, factories began to mass-produce cheap replicas of the fine crafts the Abenaki made by hand, and the Indians' income was reduced even further.

Other Abenaki took jobs as day laborers on the farms and in the paper mills that popped up on lands they had once hunted as their own. Some turned to seasonal work picking blueberries or potatoes. The logging companies that ate into the forests provided employment, too. A few Abenaki acted as guides to travelers in the area: Penobscot chief Joseph Attean guided Henry David Thoreau when the New England author ventured through the Maine woods in the 1850s. Another Penobscot, Joseph Polis, guided him on a second trip. Thoreau mentions his guides briefly in his book *The Maine Woods*.

As times grew harder, the Abenaki had no choice but to rely increasingly on whites. The U.S. government and the governments of the northeastern states—Massachusetts, Vermont, and (eventually) Maine—represented their best hope of protection in this difficult period of land loss, economic change, poverty, and painful adjustment. Unfortunately, despite some good intentions, these governments did little to help the Abenaki hold on to their land, livelihood, or tradition.

When the new United States was created, Massachusetts assumed the right to deal with the Abenaki of Maine because Maine was still part of it. (Maine became a state in 1820.) As early as 1786, the Massachusetts government pressed the Penobscot to give up their land by signing a treaty. They refused, but the pressure mounted. As it became harder and harder for the Indians to make a living, selling off part of their lands often seemed the only way for them to avoid starvation.

Some protection came from the newly formed U.S. government, which was anxious to show the world that Americans could act with humanitarian concern toward the original inhabitants of the country. The issue was underscored by unrest between Indians and whites on the frontiers. In July 1790, Congress passed the first of a series of laws "to regulate trade and intercourse with the Indian tribes." This legislation was intended to help enforce the law on the frontiers and to protect the Indians against unscrupulous whites. Section 1 of the Trade and Intercourse Act made it illegal to trade or deal with Indian tribes without a license from the U.S. government. Section 4 declared

> that no sale of lands made by any Indians, or any nation or tribe of Indians within the United States, shall be valid to any person or persons, or to any state, whether having the right of pre-emption to such lands or not, unless the same shall be made and duly executed at some public treaty, held under the authority of the United States.

Joseph Attean (son of Chief John Attean), photographed about 1855. The last lifetime chief of the Penobscot Nation, he was elected governor of the tribe at age 33. Attean worked as a lumberman and once guided the writer Henry David Thoreau on a tour of Maine.

In other words, all treaties and land sales negotiated with Indians had to be approved by the federal government. The problem was that the new federal government was not yet strong enough to enforce such laws, especially on distant frontiers where settlers acted without regard for the rights of the Indians or the wishes of the government. Thus, the Trade and Intercourse Act did little at the time to help the Abenaki. Eventually, however, it provided the legal justification for the tribe's descendants in the 1970s to reclaim their lands.

In 1794 the Passamaquoddy signed a treaty with Massachusetts, ceding to the state more than 1 million acres. The treaty was never approved by the federal government and would later be declared invalid, but at the time it cost the Passamaquoddy most of their land. This land sale left most Passamaquoddy with no place to live but at Pleasant Point reservation, in Maine. In 1796, the Penobscot signed another disastrous treaty. It called for them to yield almost 200,000 acres of their land in the Penobscot Valley in return for an annual supply of 150 yards of blue cloth; 400 pounds of shot and 100 pounds of powder; 100 bushels of corn and 13 bushels of salt; and 1 barrel of rum. They lost land on both sides of the river as far as 30 miles north of Bangor but kept the upper Penobscot Valley as hunting territory.

The depletion of beaver and the decline of the fur trade drastically reduced the Penobscots' income from their re-

maining hunting territories, however, and soon they were forced to sell more land. In 1818 John Attean—their governor, or first sagamore—sold timber from tribal lands in an effort to generate income and to help the Penobscot make ends meet. The government of Massachusetts stepped in and declared that the Indians had no right to sell the timber. Instead, the government demanded a new treaty. The Penobscot were persuaded to give up all their remaining land except for four townships and their islands in the Penobscot River. In return, Massachusetts agreed to grant annuities, or yearly payments, giving the Indians food, blankets and clothing, and powder and shot. The treaty of 1818 was illegal, however, because Congress never ratified it.

By 1820, when Maine earned statehood, the Abenaki owned only a few thousand acres out of the vast territory that had once been their homeland. They would soon lose more land. The government of Maine declared that Indians were not sovereign people but wards of the state compelled to obey its dictates. In 1833 the government paid $50,000 for the 4 Penobscot townships. The Penobscot protested that the sale was fraudulent and had been secured with false signatures, but the governor of Maine pushed the sale through. About the same time, the tribe sold five of its islands. By the middle of the century, most Penobscot were confined to Indian Island at Old Town, where they lived in a kind of ghetto separated from the white community that surrounded them.

As more and more of their territory was taken from them, the Abenaki had no choice but to ask the state for economic assistance. Some came through interest set aside by the government when it leased or sold Indian lands and through money allocated to the Indians by the state legislature. The trouble was that instead of consulting the Indians themselves about how this money should be used, the legislature turned the funds over to the local Indian agent (a white, state-appointed official who administered Indian affairs) to dispense as he chose. The agent's control of welfare payments increased the state's control over the Abenakis' lives, and the Abenaki themselves felt the shame of accepting "charity," even though the "handouts" were financed by the sale of lands they had once owned.

Other problems arose from internal divisions within the Abenaki community. Economic hardship and the ad-

This needle case, made in the 19th century, is elaborately decorated with glass beads obtained from white traders.

By the middle of the 19th century, most Penobscot remaining in Maine were confined to Indian Island at Old Town. Factional differences over religion, land, and schools weakened the tribe for decades to come, though such crafts as canoe making continued.

justment to a radically different culture led to disputes that split both the Penobscot and the Passamaquoddy into competing factions. A major issue was education. Two centuries of contact with French priests had left most Abenaki with strong attachments to the Catholic church. However, when Maine became a state Protestant ministers arrived to educate the Indians and open schools for them. Many Abenaki recognized the importance of schooling if their young people were to be able to cope in this drastically changed world. Others opposed the schools as a threat

to their culture and their Catholic religion.

Another issue concerned the Abenaki tradition of appointing chiefs who held office for life. Some Penobscot wanted to discontinue this practice because of a dispute that arose from the personal rivalry between the governor, or first sagamore, John Attean, and the lieutenant governor, or second sagamore, John Neptune. Attean's election had been controversial, and his sale of tribal timber in 1818 had aroused opposition. Neptune's behavior was, it seemed, equally erratic. The disagreement between the two men fueled a quarrel that split the tribe for many years to come.

Soon the opposing groups in both the Penobscot and the Passamaquoddy tribes divided into factions formed along family lines. One faction, the Old Party, favored Protestant schools and traditional lifetime chiefs. The other, the New Party, opposed the schools and lifetime chiefs and wanted to see the Catholic church retain its control. The dispute became so bitter that it caused a split in each tribe. Some of the New Party left the Penobscot and went to live with the Caughnawaga near Montreal. In 1851 some members of the Passamaquoddy New Party split off from the reservation at Point Pleasant and began a new village at Peter Dana Point, about 60 miles away. The Passamaquoddy have lived in two separate villages ever since.

These disputes prevented the tribal government from functioning effectively and created a vacuum that was filled by the state and its agents. The government of Maine made several attempts to mediate the dispute, finally reaching solutions that both parties could accept. The Passamaquoddy agreed to accept English as the language used in their schools as long as the teachers were still Catholic priests or nuns. On the issue of chieftainships, the Penobscot and Passamaquoddy agreed in 1866 to elect a chief from one party for one term and from the rival party two years later. In this way, life-

time chieftainships came to an end, but neither the Old nor the New Party would control the tribal government. The last lifetime chief of the Penobscot was Joseph Attean—the son of John Attean—who was chosen by the Old Party in 1858. His term ended eight years later when the Penobscot adopted the new system of choosing chiefs. The system of electing alternating chiefs lasted until 1931. Today the Penobscot elect a governor, a lieutenant governor, and 12 council members, as well as a representative to Maine's state legislature. Though the major issues were resolved, the dispute left the Penobscot and Passamaquoddy weakened and with less control over their own affairs.

The Abenaki were not alone in their disharmony. Indeed, the larger society that helped fragment them also was at odds with itself. Sectional and political conflicts in the United States led to the Civil War, fought from 1861 to 1865. A number of Penobscot and Passamaquoddy volunteered to fight for the Union, though it meant travel far from home and though the U.S. government was at first reluctant to accept them.

The Abenaki of St. Francis, Quebec, also had their share of hardship and change in the 19th century. After Robert Rogers had destroyed the village in 1759, the Abenaki built a small wooden church that included the bell they had salvaged from the first village church. In 1819 fire destroyed the second church and they had to build a third, which they did between 1828 and 1831.

Most of the inhabitants of St. Francis remained Roman Catholic, but some became Protestant after an Abenaki named Peter Paul Wzokhilain (also spelled Osunkhirhine) was appointed a missionary to the Abenaki by the American Board of Commissioners for Foreign Missions in Boston in 1835. Osunkhirhine had attended Dartmouth College in Hanover, New Hampshire, and had become a convert to the Congregationalist church (many Abenaki attended Dartmouth). A number of Abenaki followed his example after he returned home as their Congregationalist minister. In the 1860s the Anglicans also built a church at St. Francis.

A Penobscot girl at Squirrel Island, Maine, in the early 20th century. As tribes shrunk in size and local autonomy waned, few Abenaki children learned their native language.

In 1900 the third Catholic church was destroyed when it was struck by lightning, though the fire spared the sacristy built in 1828. The new century opened with the Abenaki once more rebuilding their church. Both the Anglican church and the Catholic church rebuilt in 1900 are still used by the Abenaki at St. Francis. This fourth Catholic church is adorned with beautiful wood carvings done by the Abenaki.

At the same time, changes occurred in the basketmaking industry, when dealers from Montreal, New York, and Toronto began to market the Abenaki's baskets, supplying the Indians with raw materials and distributing the finished products in the cities. The new arrangement provided the Abenaki with a steady income, and Indian families no longer needed to travel to the United States to sell their wares in the summer months.

As the 19th century drew to a close, Abenaki in Maine, Vermont, and Quebec endured more hardship and change. Disease and poverty continued to reduce their numbers. Their children attended schools where they were punished for speaking their native language. The traditional language began to die out. Penobscot and Passamaquoddy left their reservations in search of better jobs and improved living conditions, and many married outside the Indian community. Western Abenaki in Vermont remained so inconspicuous—living on marginal lands—that popular opinion held that no Indians lived in the Green Mountain state.

Louis Francis Sockalexis of the Penobscot played professional baseball in 1897–99 for the Cleveland Spiders, later renamed the Cleveland Indians in his honor.

One Penobscot Indian who made a short-lived transition into white society was Louis Francis Sockalexis, who left Old Town, Maine, to play baseball at Holy Cross College and Notre Dame. In 1897 he made it to the major leagues, breaking into the lineup of the Cleveland Spiders. In his first season he played the outfield, batted .338, and stole 16 bases. Sockalexis's career was cut short by a drinking problem, and he died in 1913 at the age of 42. In honor of his accomplishments, the Cleveland franchise changed its name to the Cleveland Indians.

Few Indians met with such achievement or acceptance in white society at the end of the 19th century, however. The prevailing view of the state and federal governments was that Indians should assimilate into white society, shed their own habits, and adopt white ways of life, education, and work. They should, in other words, abandon their own identity and merge quietly into the powerful society that had taken away most of their lands. ▲

Dark Cloud, an Abenaki who worked in a carnival sideshow before World War I. The spreading poverty among Native Americans after they lost their lands obliged some to take degrading jobs.

HARD TIMES
AND
NEW TIMES

In the early years of the 20th century, the American public seemed convinced that the Indians were doomed to extinction. In the East, only a handful survived, living as "squatters" on marginal lands. And the government seemed indifferent to the Indians' plight and problems. Eventually, reform movements took hold and federal policy changed, but these advances hardly affected life at Indian Island or at Swanton. The Abenaki continued to be ruled by poverty, prejudice, and hardship.

Even those Americans who showed concern for Indians thought they ought to assimilate into the dominant society that surrounded them. Many whites viewed the Abenaki in Maine and Vermont simply as welfare recipients and vagrants rather than as the original inhabitants of the land, with their own cherished values and unique needs. The education offered to, or imposed on, Abenaki children was calculated to

eliminate all traces of "Indianness" and replace it with the "American" language and culture. Abenaki children who dared to admit in school that they were Indian opened themselves to scorn and ridicule.

As in the 19th century, the tribe exercised almost no control over its own affairs. Elected tribal leaders had little say in the policies that affected the people's daily life: Real authority rested with the state and its agents. The federal government granted all Indians citizenship in 1924, but individual states still could—and often did—lock Indians out of the voting booth. Not until 1954 did Maine finally allow its original inhabitants to exercise their voting privileges—thus becoming the last state in the Union to do so.

The economic crisis known as the Great Depression gripped the entire nation in the 1930s and hit Indians especially hard. The few Indians who had

A Penobscot woman weaves strips of the inner bark of the basswood tree into a sturdy carrying bag. The strips are boiled with wood ashes to soften the fiber and are then shaved down to the proper width.

held steady jobs were usually the first to lose them when the depression forced employers to pare down the work force. Indians laboring in various mills, on farms, on the railroad, and for logging companies went jobless and could support themselves only by fishing and hunting. Soon these resources dwindled as well. Sharing, always a way of life among the Abenaki, became

crucial to the community's survival.

Outside their own community, the Abenaki met with little sympathy. In Maine and Vermont, even those whites similarly buffeted by the depression turned a cold eye toward Indians, whom they characterized as dirty and lazy. Once again, many Abenaki chose to conceal their identity rather than invite animosity. Concealment was relatively easy for the Abenaki in Vermont because many of them spoke French and had French-sounding names.

But the barren depression years yielded unexpected fruit as a movement begun in the 1920s to reform U.S. Indian policy gained momentum in the 1930s. The presidential election of 1932 installed an activist president in the White House, Franklin D. Roosevelt, who promised a New Deal for the American people and the "forgotten man." Roosevelt named John Collier, a longtime Indian-rights activist, as the new commissioner of Indian affairs, and federal Indian policy shifted dramatically. Collier abandoned the old notion of assimilation and, in its place, pushed for *cultural pluralism*, which meant that white society would help preserve Indian language and culture. Collier's programs called for constitutions drawn up by the tribes themselves, for better educational opportunities, and for financial and social assistance that would boost Indians up from their rung near the bottom of the social ladder.

Few of these changes visibly helped

the Abenaki, however, who continued to suffer at the hands of state lawmakers; most local officials still clearly expected and intended that the tribes should disintegrate and disappear. A bill passed by the Maine legislature in 1941, for instance, declared that an Indian who married someone of less than one-quarter Indian descent automatically ceased to be a member of the tribe. That same year, Abenaki living near Missisquoi, Vermont, found their shrinking hunting and fishing grounds curtailed more when the state set aside much of the marsh at the mouth of the Missisquoi River as a wildlife refuge.

Then, once again, war struck, and the Abenaki joined the millions of others who threw themselves into the effort to defeat Nazi Germany, and Japan, which attacked the American naval base at Pearl Harbor, Hawaii, on December 7, 1941. Some 25,000 American Indians, including members of the Abenaki tribe, fought in World War II. Others worked in war-related industries away from their reservations.

Indians who returned from the war brought with them new expectations. But few were prepared for the federal government's reverse course on Indian policy in the late 1940s and 1950s. The new program, known as *termination*, called for policymakers to, in effect, "get out of the Indian business." The government abandoned its support of tribal cultures and readopted the policy of assimilation. It wanted to end federal services and withdraw protection for

Franklin D. Roosevelt, elected president in 1932, promised a "New Deal" for the "forgotten man." His policies helped improve the social and financial conditions of Native Americans.

Indian people. In some areas of the country, Indian tribes were simply declared "terminated"; others were relocated away from their reservations to live in the cities.

In 1951–52 a legislative research committee in Maine advocated support for the federal government's new policies. The committee recommended that Indian children continue to be educated in white schools, and it encouraged the state to purchase reservation lands.

ABENAKI PLACE NAMES

Many names used by the Abenaki to describe places and geographical features in their homeland have remained in use. The following list is selected from Maine, Vermont, and New Hampshire.

Androscoggin	place where fish are cured
Ashuelot	place between
Coös/Cowass	place of pine trees
Connecticut	the long river
Katahdin	the principal mountain
Kennebec	long water without rapids
Memphremagog	where there is a great expanse of water
Merrimack	at the deep place
Missisquoi	place of the flint, or the great grassy meadows
Nashua	between streams
Piscataqua	where the river divides
Sagadahoc	the outflowing of a swift stream as it nears the sea
Umbagog Lake	clear lake
Wawenock	bay country, or inlet places

These and many more Abenaki place names are identified in John C. Huden's *Indian Place Names of New England* (New York: Museum of the American Indian, Heye Foundation, 1962.)

The death knell evidently was sounded for the Abenaki in 1951, when a bridge was built linking the mainland to the Penobscot on Indian Island. Four-time governor of Indian Island, Francis Ranco, recalled that the bridge changed everything, destroying the quiet that had once characterized life on Indian Island. Paved roads made horses obsolete. Young Penobscots lost the few remaining vestiges of tradition, basketmaking declined, and the native language was silenced to the point where, in Ranco's words, "Parents don't speak Indian anymore and their children just never learn it."

Some admirers of Abenaki culture, aware that it was in danger of disappearing, devoted themselves to learning and recording as much as they could of existing tribal life. Luckily, a few students of Indian life had been at work for a long time. One such scholar was Frank G. Speck, an anthropologist at the University of Pennsylvania, who in the first four decades of the 20th century had documented the vitality of Native American culture. He gathered a mass of information on the Algonquian peoples of the East, and he paid particular attention to the Penobscot, taking many photographs and writing extensively about their life and culture. In the 1950s, Gordon M. Day of the Canadian Ethnology Service began his linguistic and historical studies at Odanak, and this project brought the western Abenaki to the attention of serious scholars.

These efforts helped enlighten the public and also policymakers, who gradually realized that a vital part of American culture was about to vanish. Just as it seemed that the light of Abenaki identity was about to be snuffed out, it began to burn brighter. In the 1950s, when the state of Maine increased the pressure on its Indians to assimilate, Penobscot and Passamaquoddy spokesmen became more vocal in opposing these policies. There remained, however, some disagreement within the tribe about the best course of action. Some people resented being dependent on the state and thought that living and working in white society offered a means of escape from the poverty on the reservations. But a growing number of Abenaki actively opposed the government's policies of assimilation. A new spirit of pride arose among the Indians.

In part because they were scarcely recognized for their contributions in the American Revolution and the Civil War, the Abenaki installed this memorial at Odanak, Quebec, to their soldiers in the two world wars.

Indian reformers spoke out against the government's attempt to destroy the tribes. Their argument was built on the assertion that the state had no right to pass laws affecting the Indians' life. In 1949, Penobscot and Passamaquoddy alike petitioned for the removal of Indian agent Hiram Hall. They resented his authoritarian attitude, his refusal to consult them on issues that changed their life, and his high-handed manner of doling out state aid. The petition failed, however, and Hall remained in office until 1965. Other reform proposals made no more headway.

Indian leaders grew convinced that they needed to take control of their own affairs and their own resources. They pressed for rights that, though guaranteed by treaty, had been denied them for generations. Most important, they considered reclaiming some of the lands that had been taken away from them by treaty.

In 1957 the Penobscot held a tribal meeting to draw up plans for regaining their tribal sovereignty. In a deliberate move to demonstrate their determination to revive and retain the old ways, they changed their leader's title from tribal governor to tribal chief. They also demanded official recognition as a sep-

By the time this bridge from the mainland to Indian Island, Maine, was built in 1951, most Abenaki were largely isolated from white America. A second bridge was built in 1988.

This 1919 photograph of Abenaki living in the White Mountains of New Hampshire was taken by anthropologist Frank G. Speck, who diligently studied Indian life and culture for 40 years.

arate nation, and in 1958, in a symbolic move to assert their sovereign status, they even selected their own delegates to the United Nations.

These initial efforts met with little success, and the Indians' victories were small. But they halted the political wheels that had been crushing them for so long. By the end of the 1950s, Maine had begun to take Indian demands seriously and responded with some improvements. In 1959, for example, the state granted free hunting and fishing licenses to all members of the Penobscot

and Passamaquoddy tribes. In addition, the Penobscot were authorized to pass and enforce their own local ordinances. The drive to terminate the tribes was grinding to a halt; the Abenaki had turned the tide.

The 1960s was a decade of turbulent change for American society as a whole, and Indians belonged to a growing population of dissidents that included blacks, students, and opponents of the Vietnam War. Federal policymakers revised the way Indian affairs were conducted, and tribes secured more control

*The slogan Red Power became a byword of
the civil-rights movement of the 1960s as
Indians in the United States and Canada
voiced their grievances. The fight continues—these Canadian citizens staged a tribal
ceremony at the United Nations in 1980.*

over their own affairs. Indians took up
the slogan Red Power. And in 1968, mil-
itant Indians, including some Abenaki,
formed the American Indian Movement
(AIM).

The major issues in the 1960s for the
Abenaki of Maine and Vermont remained economic. Income was low and
unemployment was still extremely
high—as much as 75 percent of the po-

tential work force had no jobs. Poverty
and prejudice limited the opportunities
for Abenaki children, and many families still lived in houses that lacked
plumbing and electricity. But now the
tribe had hope.

In 1965, Maine became the first state
to establish its own Department of Indian Affairs, after having neglected its
natives for so long. The department's
purpose was to provide financial assistance, administer services on the reservations, and initiate "programs
aimed at human and community development . . . based on expressed
needs of the Indian people." The state
acknowledged that its assimilation policy had failed. It would now deal with
the Indians as distinct communities
with their own special concerns and
their own unique heritage. Indians
themselves geared up for a new era,
too. They formed two new organizations, the Association of Aroostook Indians and the Central Maine Indian
Association, to help the many Indians
in Maine who did not live on reservations.

In 1962 the name of the Abenaki reserve near Pierreville, Quebec, was officially changed to Odanak. Most
Abenaki there spoke French as a first
language and worked outside the reservation. Basketmaking was no longer
an important economic activity, and
children attended white schools. But
the Abenaki had not forgotten the old
ways. In the early 1960s, with the help
of missionary J. Remi Dolan, they es-

tablished the *Musée des Abenakis* (Abenaki Museum) at Odanak. The museum houses an impressive collection of displays, basketry, and other artifacts, as well as documents testifying to the rich heritage of the Abenaki people of Quebec.

These developments were encouraging, but the Indians had further to go. Until they controlled their own natural and financial resources, they would always be dependent on—and limited by—the state. The key to independence was ownership, but few Abenaki had enough money to feed their family, let alone to invest in real estate. Then, in the late 1960s, the Passamaquoddy initiated a lawsuit to regain thousands of acres for the Indians of Maine. The suit would culminate in a landmark decision, ushering in a new era in American-Indian relations. ▲

Penobscot boys on Indian Island, Maine, a town that like other Abenaki communities has enjoyed an economic and cultural revival since the mid-1970s.

THE
ABENAKI
TODAY

In the 1970s many American Indians turned to violent protest to call attention to their plight and to assert control over their own affairs. Others fought their battles in the courts, basing their cases on the rights promised them by treaties and on laws broken generations before. For some groups, this was a time to stand up and declare their heritage, to demand that society recognize them as Indians. The Abenaki, ignored for so long, forced the United States to take them into account.

The Passamaquoddy and Penobscot chose the courtroom as their battlefield. A young white lawyer named Thomas Tureen, who was interested in Indian and civil-rights issues, took up the tribes' cause and managed it through a 10-year legal battle.

As he reviewed the Passamaquoddies' claims, Tureen decided they should base their case on the Trade and Intercourse Act. This law, passed in 1790, stipulated that all transfers of Indian lands must be approved by Congress. The official government position had long been that the law's restrictions did not apply to states—such as Maine—that were not among the original 13 states or to Indian tribes not recognized by the federal government. (Federal recognition means that the U.S. government has a "trust" relationship with an Indian tribe or, in other words, that it is obligated by treaty or other agreements to protect that tribe's interests.)

Tureen believed that the act *did* apply in Maine and in every state and that the treaties made after 1790 by Massachusetts and Maine with the Passamaquoddy and Penobscot, which had never received federal approval, were invalid. Consequently, all sales of land that resulted from the treaties were illegal. On the basis of this argument, the Passamaquoddy and the Penobscot

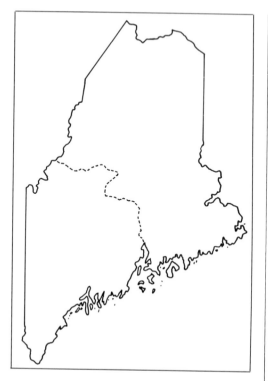

The part of Maine north and east of the line, about two-thirds of the state, is roughly the land that the Passamaquoddy and Penobscot claimed had been taken from them illegally since the 1600s. In 1975 the tribes won a protracted legal battle over the land.

brought suit for the return of lands constituting more than two-thirds of the state of Maine.

The Indians knew that landowners in Maine were not about to hand over their property. In 1971, Tureen enlisted the support of NARF (the Native American Rights Fund, founded in 1970 to advocate Indian interests), and the Passamaquoddy and Penobscot dug in for

a long legal fight. Secretary of the Interior Rogers C. B. Morton refused to provide lawyers to undertake the suit, arguing that the tribes did not fall under the government's trust responsibilities. So the Indians sued in the federal district court in Maine. In January 1975, in the case of *Passamaquoddy Tribe v. Morton*, Judge Edward T. Gignoux ruled that even though the tribe had never been federally recognized, the Trade and Intercourse Act did apply to them and that the act had in fact established a trust relationship between the United States and the Passamaquoddy.

Gignoux's decision created a precedent and opened a breach through which Indian groups that had not been formally recognized as tribes might sue for return of lands lost by treaty. In Maine the decision created widespread alarm and cast a cloud over many land titles. Were the land sales invalid? Would people have their land taken away from them by a court ruling that declared it belonged to the Indians? White landowners were outraged, the governor of Maine accused the Indians of blackmail, and angry whites who feared they might lose their homes threatened and harassed their Indian neighbors.

In 1977, President Jimmy Carter asked for a special report evaluating the Penobscot and Passamaquoddy claims. On the basis of that report, and on his understanding that a long, drawn-out court fight would cause irreparable damage and ill feeling in Maine, the president advocated an out-of-court settlement. He appointed a White House task force to meet with the 11-man negotiating committee of the Penobscot and Passamaquoddy and work out a settlement. The negotiators issued a joint memorandum early in 1978, but strong opposition, political pressure, and technical hitches delayed implementation of their agreement.

Finally, in March 1980 a settlement was reached and was approved by the Passamaquoddy and Penobscot as well as by the Houlton Band of Maliseet In-

dians. In June, Maine's two senators introduced the proposal to Congress, and on October 10, 1980, President Carter, using an eagle-feather pen, signed the Maine Indian Claims Settlement Act into law.

The new law validated all the land sales that the Indians had made in the past, thereby reassuring white landowners that they were not about to lose their property. In return, the Indians won a settlement of $81.5 million from the federal government. Congress established a $27 million trust fund to be

In 1980 President Jimmy Carter signed a bill—with an eagle-feather pen—granting the Passamaquoddy and Penobscot $81.5 million as restitution for the loss of their lands.

administered by the Interior Department for the benefit of the Indian tribes of Maine. The remaining $54.5 million was set aside for the Maine Indian Claims Land Acquisition Fund to repurchase 300,000 acres. The Penobscot and Passamaquoddy were granted federal recognition and were declared eligible to receive all the health and welfare services the federal government provided for other Indian tribes. The settlement was the largest victory of its kind in American history.

Having won this hard-fought battle, the Penobscot and Passamaquoddy were not about to let the fruits of their victory spoil. Other tribes that had won large legal settlements had divided the money among tribal members on a *per capita* basis (disbursing the cash equally to every member), with the result that the tribe as a whole often had little or nothing left for investment, for social programs, and for economic development. As former Penobscot governor Timothy Love said, "We just did not want to dissipate all our money the way some other Indians have with their settlements." In Maine, the Indians were determined that their victory should provide a foundation on which to build a future.

Indeed, one victory has followed another since the settlement. The tribes applied their award toward achieving long-range economic self-sufficiency, first by repurchasing 300,000 acres of forestland. In addition, the trust fund established by the Settlement Act gives

Thomas N. Tureen served as attorney for the Indians of Maine in the 1975 land-claims case. He later became their investment adviser.

each Penobscot and Passamaquoddy family about $1,000 each year. The most significant investments were made to reduce unemployment, to generate income, and to bolster the tribes' economic independence. Thomas Tureen continued to serve the Penobscot and Passamaquoddy as a financial adviser, and the Penobscot formed an investment committee. The Passamaquoddy bought a large blueberry farm near Machias, where many of them had previously worked as pickers, and now run it as a tribal business; in 1988 it was the largest independent producer of commercially grown blueberries in the state.

The Passamaquoddy also paid about $25 million for the various parts of the Dragon Products Company, New England's only cement maker; to make the acquisition, the tribe leveraged its assets, leased the plant, bought out the lease, and employed other sophisticated financial tactics. Then, in July 1988, the tribe's assets-management firm sold Dragon Products for an estimated $80 million. Unlike most previous business deals made by Indian tribes, this sale did not include any guarantee of jobs for Indians—profit was the sole motive, though the cement plant's new owners will continue to employ Indians. The *New York Times* said the sale showed the Indians "wheeling and dealing like a Wall Street investment firm." The $80 million will be used for other investments, and part of it could also be disbursed to individuals. The real point of this maneuvering, however, is to assure the preservation of their culture, for the Passamaquoddy also own a bilingual radio station and run a bilingual education program whose goal is to guarantee that young people have the opportunity to learn their native language as well as English. Individual Passamaquoddies have not become millionaires overnight. Rather, the tribe will be able to live on.

On Indian Island, 12 miles north of Bangor, the Penobscot built Sockalexis Memorial Ice Arena at a cost of $1.5 million. They hoped Maine's various minor-league hockey teams would use the facilities, but the demand for the arena did not meet the tribe's expectations. New plans call for other uses of the arena, possibly to serve as a bingo hall that would bring additional income and employment to Indian Island. The Penobscot helped construct a factory that makes audiocassettes and provides many jobs and generates income for the tribe. Other projects included an impressive new school, a community center, and high-quality housing for tribe members. A new two-lane bridge from Indian Island to the mainland promises to make communication easier between the reservation and the outside world. The Penobscot also run a tourist camp on their lands.

These developments have not blinded the tribe to the need for preserving traditional culture. In 1988, a dictionary of the Penobscot language was nearing publication, and the Penobscot school offered instruction in native arts and language. The community planned to establish a new cultural center, together with the tribal museum and library, in the island's old schoolhouse. In 1988, out of a total Penobscot population of about 2,000, some 550 people lived on Indian Island, one of the tribe's 146 islands.

The recent achievements of the Penobscot and Passamaquoddy stand as an

Indian Island, Maine, in 1972. The island is 1 of 146 islands owned by the Penobscot, and as home to 550 of the tribe's 2,000 members it is the focal point of their activity.

example to other tribes. Sound investment and careful planning for the future have enabled these tribes to seize control of their own destiny. They have proved that Indian tribes can succeed in business without losing their heritage and can emerge as important contributors to the very state that ignored them for centuries.

The Abenaki of Vermont have also taken steps both to gain a foothold on the future and to keep their heritage alive. For many generations, this branch of the Abenaki people had lived in small family bands located near their traditional lands at Missisquoi, where they kept a low profile. But things changed in the 1970s. The protests and activism of that decade prompted the Vermont Abenaki to strengthen their sense of unity and to assert more control over their own affairs. They formed a tribal council, reconstituted the St. Francis–Sokoki Band of the Abenaki Nation of Vermont, and established headquarters in an old railroad depot in Swanton. Soon more than 1,000 persons registered as members of the tribe.

In 1976 the Abenaki living at Odanak and Becancour, followed by the Quebec Federation of Indians and the U.S. Federal Regional Task Force, all recognized the Abenaki of Vermont and requested the state of Vermont to do the same. The Vermont Abenaki also petitioned the state to grant them exemption from its hunting and fishing regulations.

On Thanksgiving Day in 1976, Governor Thomas Salmon issued an executive order granting state recognition to the Abenaki of Vermont, but the newly elected Republican governor, Richard Snelling, pressured by organized sport-fishing groups, revoked the order when he took office in 1977. Bitterly disappointed, the Abenaki realized that they would have to take their demand for recognition to the federal government. The tribal council drew up a written constitution that provided for elections to tribal office and outlined the power of the council and chief. The council then set about the costly and lengthy process of persuading the federal government to recognize them as an Indian tribe.

The western Abenaki of Vermont have not received as much attention as the eastern Abenaki of Maine, but they too are persevering in the effort to revive their culture. Shown here is the tribal council hall of the western Abenaki, in Swanton, Vermont.

Because the Vermont Abenaki had never signed a treaty with the United States, they had to prove their identity to the Bureau of Indian Affairs (BIA). This procedure called for the tribe to demonstrate its *aboriginal occupancy*, or ancient and uninterrupted residence in a specific location. It was no easy task to prove aboriginal occupancy—the tribe had managed to survive precisely because it tried hard not to be visible. As a result, it took the Vermont Abenaki many years of research and much expense to acquire the necessary information and documentation to prove long-standing residence there. In 1982 the tribe submitted its petition for federal recognition; in 1988 it was still awaiting a decision from the BIA.

In 1988 some 2,000 Abenaki lived in Vermont. The largest community resided in and around the Swanton, Highgate, and St. Albans area. These people still suffer from low income, high unemployment, and inadequate educational opportunities. They also endure taunts from those who claim they are not "real Indians." Federal recognition would mean that the Vermont Abenaki could qualify for government assistance programs as an Indian tribe. It would also confirm that they were the original occupants of Vermont, a people who have held on to their homeland despite all the pressures to abandon it.

The Vermont Abenaki have not passively awaited government aid. Under the guidance of Chief Leonard Lampman and then Homer St. Francis, they have used their revived unity and their renewed sense of pride to take their own steps toward improvement. They have staged fish-ins—fishing out of season and without licenses on the Missisquoi River—in order to publicize their claim to special status in their traditional territory. In 1976 they created the Abenaki Self Help Association, Inc. (ASHAI) to set about bettering their lot. The ASHAI initiated many programs. Some provided food, better housing, and improved health. Others funded social and educational programs that supported local businesses and combated poverty. Still others sought to reduce prejudice, to create opportunities for young Abenaki, and to foster pride in the Abenaki heritage.

The western Abenaki have demanded the return of excavated Abenaki remains for proper reburial in ancestral sites and have blocked developers from excavating burial grounds. In 1988, Chief Homer St. Francis demanded that the U.S. Fish and Wildlife Service vacate the Missisquoi National Wildlife Refuge and return the land to the tribe. Whether or not the BIA decides to recognize them as an Indian tribe, the Abenaki in Vermont, like the Penobscot and Passamaquoddy in Maine, have shown they will take charge of their life and work to shape their future.

The status of Indians in Canada is rather different from that of Indians in the United States. The Canadian government distinguishes between four separate groups of native peoples: (1) status Indians, native people who are registered under the Indian Act; (2) nonstatus Indians, native people who identify themselves as Indians but who are not registered for the purposes of the Indian Act; (3) Metis, people of Euro-Indian descent; and (4) Inuits (Eskimos). Whereas the United States grants or withholds recognition to an Indian *tribe* and allows the tribe to determine its membership, in Canada *individuals* are assigned status on the basis of lineage and entered in the Indian Register. Indians with registered ancestors can become status Indians. Because the Canadian government assigns status to individual Indians rather than to bands or tribes, it is possible for some tribe members to live as band members on a reserve even though they do not yet qualify as status Indians. But 99 percent of the Indian peoples of Canada who are band members are registered

In an attempt to gain approval for special privileges on their historic waters and lands, members of the St. Francis–Sokoki Band of the Abenaki Nation of Vermont have fished without licenses in protests called fish-ins.

This burial site in Newbury, Vermont, honors the memory of a man who fought alongside the colonists in the American Revolution.

as status Indians. The Abenaki in Quebec are registered and therefore are regarded as status Indians.

In 1982 the Abenaki at Odanak established the Mikwobait Cultural Association, designed to preserve Abenaki culture and heritage. In 1983 they started a profit-making corporation to create permanent employment for craft workers. The corporation produces clothes, baskets, and ornaments and sells them through outlets in Quebec, Montreal, and some cities in the United States. In this way, traditional handicrafts are encouraged and jobs are provided. The Abenaki Museum continues to attract visitors from around the world, and each July the Abenaki of Odanak hold a festival of art, dancing, and singing. About 200 people live in the Odanak community, with some 600 in the band as a whole. Another 100 or so live at Becancour, which in 1983 became known as Wôlinak.

The Abenaki have survived some 400 years of contact with the Europeans and Americans who invaded their homeland. Over the centuries, war and disease have thinned their numbers and they have seen their lands taken away from them. Many migrated from their homelands in search of refuge; others have intermarried with non-Indians and assumed the outward appearance of white Americans or Canadians. They have seen their independence threatened, their culture attacked, and their identity questioned. At times they seemed about to disappear.

Yet even in the worst of times, the Abenaki people have clung to their heritage and their belief in themselves. Since the late 1960s, they have steadily restored their cultural base and compelled their neighbors and the world to look at them in a new light.

More work lies ahead for this tribe, however. Poverty and prejudice cannot be wiped out overnight, and new problems surface daily. In the late 1980s the Penobscot joined a chorus of Indian tribes who objected to U.S. Department of Energy proposals to bury nuclear waste on their reservations. No doubt more difficulties will emerge as the Abenaki struggle both to deal with the outside world and to remain intact as Indians with their own history, culture, and values. But as long as they stay unified as a people and receive fair treatment from national and local government, the Abenaki will meet new challenges, just as they have met them for hundreds of years. ▲

BIBLIOGRAPHY

Anastas, Peter. *Glooskap's Children: Encounters with the Penobscot Indians of Maine*. Boston: Beacon Press, 1973.

Bennett, Dean B., ed. *Maine Dirigo: "I Lead."* Camden, ME: Down East Books, 1980.

Brodeur, Paul. *Restitution: The Land Claims of the Mashpee, Passamaquoddy, and Penobscot Indians of New England*. Boston: Northeastern University Press, 1985.

Bruchac, Joseph. *The Wind Eagle and Other Abenaki Stories as Told by Joseph Bruchac*. Illustrated by Kahionhes. Greenfield Center, NY: Bowman Books, 1985.

Calloway, Colin G. "Green Mountain Diaspora: Indian Population Movements in Vermont, c. 1600–1800." *Vermont History* 54 (Fall 1986): 197–228.

Day, Gordon M. *The Identity of the St. Francis Indians*. Ottawa, Ontario: National Museum of Canada, 1981.

————. "Western Abenaki." In *Handbook of North American Indians*, Vol. 15, *Northeast*, edited by Bruce G. Trigger. Washington, D.C.: Smithsonian Institution, 1978.

Eckstorm, Fannie Hardy. *Old John Neptune and Other Maine Indian Shamans*. Portland, ME: The Southworth-Anthoenson Press, 1945.

Finding One's Way: The Story of an Abenaki Child. Franklin, VT: Northwest Supervisory Union Title IV Indian Education Program and the Abenaki Self-Help Association, 1986.

Haviland, William A., and Marjory W. Power. *The Original Vermonters: Native Inhabitants, Past and Present*. Hanover, NH: University Press of New England, 1981.

Snow, Dean. "Eastern Abenaki." In *Handbook of North American Indians*, Vol. 15, *Northeast*, edited by Bruce G. Trigger. Washington, D.C.: Smithsonian Institution, 1978.

Speck, Frank G. *Penobscot Man: The Life History of a Forest Tribe in Maine*. Philadelphia: University of Pennsylvania Press, 1940.

THE ABENAKI AT A GLANCE

COMMONLY CALLED *Abenaki*

ORIGINAL NAME *Wabanaki*

CURRENT LOCATIONS *northern New England; southeastern Quebec*

LINGUISTIC FAMILY *Algonquian*

TRADITIONAL ECONOMY *hunting, fishing, agriculture*

FIRST EUROPEAN CONTACT *European fishermen in the 15th century; Giovanni da Verrazano, 1524*

HOMELAND AT FIRST CONTACT *northern New England*

TRADITIONAL POPULATION AT FIRST CONTACT *western Abenaki, about 10,000; eastern Abenaki, about 10,000–20,000*

SELF-IDENTIFIED POPULATION TODAY *Vermont Abenaki, about 2,000; Quebec Abenaki, about 1,000; Penobscot, about 2,000; Passamaquoddy, about 2,500*

MODERN STATUS
Canada *Abenaki in Quebec registered as "status Indians"*
United States *Penobscot recognized by federal government; Vermont Abenaki not recognized: Their petition for recognition is pending.*

GLOSSARY

Algonquian The languages spoken by most of the Indian peoples living in the northeastern United States and eastern-central Canada. Tribes that spoke these related languages include the Micmac, Shawnee, Delaware, Ojibwa, Cree, and Cheyenne.

American Indian Movement (AIM) The most radical of the modern Indian-rights groups, especially in the late 1960s and early 1970s.

artifact Any object made by human beings, such as a tool, a canoe, a garment, or an ornament.

band A loosely organized group of people who live in one area, bound together by the need for food and defense, family ties, or other common interests.

colony In the context of 17th-century North America, an area occupied and used by people from another country who remain subject to control by that country. Britain and France had colonies in Abenaki lands.

confederacy A usually temporary agreement between tribes to pursue a mutual goal. In the 17th and early 18th centuries the Abenaki took part in a confederacy of New England tribes to resist the advance of English settlers.

contact period The 16th through 18th centuries, when European explorers, traders, and settlers in North America first encountered Indians. For some eastern Abenaki, first contact took place in the early 16th century.

culture The learned behavior of human beings; nonbiological social activities; the way of life of a given group of people.

cultural pluralism Toleration and respect by a dominant society for the different cultures of other social or ethnic groups.

federal recognition The national government's legal acknowledgment of a group of people as an Indian tribe, and the subsequent provision of the services for which recognized Indian tribes are eligible.

immunity An inherited or acquired resistance to a given disease.

Jesuit A member of the Society to Jesus, a Roman Catholic order founded by Saint Ignatius Loyola

in 1534. The Jesuits are highly learned and in the 17th century were particularly active in spreading Christianity outside of Europe.

longhouse A domed structure made of tree trunks and bark that is more permanent than a wigwam. The roof has holes to let smoke escape. Abenaki longhouses could accomodate up to 60 people.

Puritan A member of a group of English Protestants who wanted simpler church ceremonies and stricter religious discipline. Puritans were particularly influential in shaping society in colonial New England.

relocation The attempt on the part of the federal government to encourage Indians to leave the tribal environment of the reservation and migrate to the cities in order to enter mainstream society.

reservation A tract of land set aside by the U.S. government specifically for occupation and use by Indians. Usually called a *reserve* in Canada.

ritual A ceremony or series of procedures, usually with religious significance.

sachem or **sagamore** A tribal ruler or chief. The word comes from the Narraganset dialect of New England and was applied by Europeans to chiefs of non-Iroquois tribes in the Northeast.

shaman A person who has special powers to call on various spirits to solve problems, heal the sick, or ensure success in acquiring food or in other essential activities; also called a *medicine man*.

smallpox An acute, contagious disease marked by skin eruptions that become scars and by chills that lead to fever, pneumonia, and usually death. The virus, a chief cause of death among American Indians in the 16th–19th centuries, has now been eradicated.

squatters Persons who occupy and live on a plot of land without having legal title to it. In the 19th century, some Abenaki were accused of squatting on land they had given up by treaty.

termination Policy of the U.S. government, begun under President Dwight D. Eisenhower in 1953, that was intended to eliminate Indian tribal and communal organizations, remove federal supervision, and end the services provided to tribes by the federal government. The policy was gradually dropped in the mid-1960s.

totem The emblem or symbol of a clan or family, usually the animal with which the family has a special or ancestral relationship.

tribe A term used to describe a community or group of related communities that share a common language, culture, and territory.

trust-status tribe The term for a tribe that has been federally recognized. Once a tribe achieves this status, the federal government is responsible for providing it with social, medical, and educational services and for protecting the tribe's right to self-government and any trust property.

vision quest A fast and vigil undertaken by Indian boys (sometimes by girls) in the hope of receiving a sign from a supernatural power who might guide and protect the youth through life. The vigil usually required extended solitude outdoors.

wampum Beads made from the white and purple parts of clam and oyster shells. They were used in strings or belts as a pledge of the truth of one's words, for symbols of high office, or as records of negotiations, treaties, and other important events. From the Algonquian word *wampumpeag*, meaning white (bead) strings.

wigwam A one-room dwelling constructed of a framework of saplings or branches covered with mats or birchbark.

PICTURE CREDITS

COLIN G. CALLOWAY was born in Yorkshire, England, and is a British citizen. He received his B.A. and Ph.D. degrees from the University of Leeds and taught for several years at the College of Ripon and York St. John. After moving to the United States, he taught high school in Vermont before serving as editor/assistant director of the D'Arcy McNickle Center for the History of the American Indian at the Newberry Library in Chicago. His first book was *Crown and Calumet: British-Indian Relations 1783–1815*, and he has written many articles on Indian history. He is currently assistant professor of history at the University of Wyoming, where he teaches American Indian history, and is writing a book on the history of the western Abenaki of Vermont.

FRANK W. PORTER III, general editor of INDIANS OF NORTH AMERICA, is director of the Chelsea House Foundation for American Indian Studies. He holds a B.A., M.A., and Ph.D. from the University of Maryland. He has done extensive research concerning the Indians of Maryland and Delaware and is the author of numerous articles on their history, archaeology, geography, and ethnography. He was formerly director of the Maryland Commission on Indian Affairs and American Indian Research and Resource Institute, Gettysburg, Pennsylvania, and he has received grants from the Delaware Humanities Forum, the Maryland Committee for the Humanities, the Ford Foundation, and the National Endowment for the Humanities, among others. Dr. Porter is the author of *The Bureau of Indian Affairs* in the Chelsea House KNOW YOUR GOVERNMENT series.